WISDOM *FOR* LIFE

A 31-DAY DEVOTIONAL
IN PROVERBS

by DOUG BATCHELOR

Wisdom for Life:
A 31-Day Devotional in Proverbs

Published by Amazing Facts, Inc.
P. O. Box 1058
Roseville, CA 95678-8058
800-538-7275
amazingfacts.org

Managing Editor: Anthony Lester
Editors: Curtis Rittenour and Laurie Lyon
Cover design and art direction by Eric Smalling
Text design by Greg Solie • Altamont Graphics

ISBN 978-1-580-19586-7

CONTENTS

INTRODUCTION

"And Solomon loved the Lord." —Proverbs 1:7

L iving successfully requires wisdom. So with God's help over the next 31 days, we will be learning about wisdom from one of the very best in the field.

King Solomon is widely known for his phenomenal wisdom, unsurpassed wealth, succinct proverbs, eloquent poetry, and his famous love song. Some believe he was wise because he had a head start genetically. After all, his father was King David and his mother, Bathsheba, was the granddaughter of Ahithophel, the wisest of David's counselors. But the Scriptures are clear that a profound wisdom specially settled upon him after he humbly solicited God for understanding (1 Kings 3:6–9).

The good news is that you can drink from the same fountain of wisdom as Solomon. "The fear of the Lord is the beginning of wisdom; a good understanding have all those who do His commandments" (Psalm 111:10).

As long as Solomon loved the Lord and sought after Him, God blessed him with supernatural wisdom, so that Israel experienced their greatest days of national glory under his wise rule. He built the magnificent temple of Jehovah, and the people lived in peace and unrivaled prosperity.

Of course, the Scriptures do record a sad episode in Solomon's history in which he seriously drifted away from God. He began to put his love for his pagan wives before his love for the Lord. When that happened, his wisdom diminished and the associated blessings began to also evaporate. But God is good. At the conclusion of Solomon's life, he was rebuked by a prophet, repented, and returned to the Lord. The book of Ecclesiastes records his repentance and the vanity of a life apart from God.

This one-month devotional is drawn from the 31 chapters of Proverbs. (It conveniently matches up with several months that contain 31 days.) Each morning and evening meditation considers a couple of choice verses from that day's chapter. To get the most from this book, I encourage you to read one of the chapters each day along with these devotionals. For example, on January 14, you could read Proverbs chapter 14 plus the morning and evening devotions found in this book. Naturally, this devotional can also be used any time of year to study the greatness and wisdom of God.

"If any of you lacks wisdom, let him ask of God, who gives to all liberally and without reproach, and it will be given to him" (James 1:5). May God bless your journey through the extraordinary riches of the Proverbs!

—Doug Batchelor

DAY I

Wisdom Verse

*"The fear of the LORD is the beginning of knowledge, but
fools despise wisdom and instruction." —Proverbs 1:7*

AN AMAZING FACT: Sixteen-year-old Andrew Kamal holds the record
for the highest IQ score ever recorded. His score of 295 makes him the
most gifted child prodigy in the world. But a high IQ does not always
translate into wisdom.

The Bible tells us that Solomon was the wisest person who ever
lived. Soon after taking the throne, the dedicated young king
earnestly prayed for God's help to govern the kingdom. During
the night the Lord revealed Himself to Solomon and said, "Ask! What
shall I give you?" (1 Kings 3:5). Can you imagine receiving an invitation
like that from the Creator of the universe? It was like receiving a blank
check. Have you ever pondered what you would do if you were given a
billion dollars?

King Solomon humbly responded to the Lord, "O LORD my God, You
have made Your servant king instead of my father David, but I am a little
child; I do not know how to go out or come in." Then he asked, "Now give
me wisdom and knowledge, that I may go out and come in before this
people; for who can judge this great people of Yours?" (2 Chronicles 1:10).

God was pleased that Solomon had not asked for fortunes, long life,
or even the death of his enemies. He said, "Behold, I have done according
to your words; see, I have given you a wise and understanding heart, so
that there has not been anyone like you before you, nor shall any like
you arise after you" (v. 12). In fact, the Lord said that even though the

young king had not asked for riches or honor, these would be given to him anyway, along with a long life ...

... But there was a condition. "If you walk in My ways, to keep My statues and My commandments, as your father David walked, then I will lengthen your days" (v. 14).

Solomon put the kingdom and righteousness of God first, and God blessed him with all the other things. This is what Jesus says will also happen if we have our priorities straight—"Seek first the kingdom of God and His righteousness, and all these things shall be added to you" (Matthew 6:33).

The wisdom of Solomon, which comes from God, can be yours today. We, too, may humbly come before the Lord with faith and seek a discerning mind. In fact, that is the whole purpose of the book of Proverbs, penned primarily by this wise man. Such wisdom comes through faith and humility. "The fear of the Lord" means that we recognize our great dependence on God for all wisdom and knowledge.

> *Thank you, heavenly Father, for answering the*
> *prayer of Solomon. Please hear my own humble*
> *cry for instruction and guidance today.*

TODAY'S MORNING READING: Proverbs 1:1–19

DAY 1

Wisdom Verse

"Wisdom calls aloud outside; she raises her voice in the open squares. She cries out in the chief concourses, at the openings of the gates in the city she speaks her words." —Proverbs 1:20

AN AMAZING FACT: The 1883 super volcanic eruption of Mount Krakatoa in Indonesia created the loudest explosion in recorded history. It was heard 3,000 miles away!

Have you ever tried to get someone's attention in a noisy crowd? Often while waiting for a person at an air terminal, I'll watch tired passengers walk into the waiting lounge. Waving signs doesn't always get people's attention. Sometimes a group of people will shout and cheer when a person steps into the room. I've occasionally whistled or shouted a friend's name above the clamor in order to be heard.

Solomon personifies wisdom in this evening's Bible passage as a woman calling to busy people rushing through public places. She raises her voice not only to be heard by them, but also to express an urgent message. It reminds me of the prophet Isaiah's message from God: "When I called, you did not answer; when I spoke, you did not hear, but did evil before My eyes" (Isaiah 65:12).

Just as the Israelites in Isaiah's day thought everything was just fine, so also the people in Solomon's time rushed through life not realizing how much they scorned God's wisdom and turned away from godly counsel. They were too preoccupied with their occupations.

"I don't have time to stop and listen to you; please get out of my way—I'm in a hurry!"

Unfortunately, when God's people refused to hear His words, the Babylonians came and destroyed their city. Many lives were lost because they were too stubborn to listen to the wisdom of God crying out to them. They resented her outstretched hand. Calamity came to people who insisted that everything was all right. Could that happen in our day?

God is still trying to get our attention. The Lord has warned us through signs in the natural and political world that earth's final events are now unfolding. Unless we learn to stop each day and listen to the quiet voice of the Holy Spirit, speaking to us through Scripture and helping us to discern the cosmic conflict happening all around us, we also will hurry past wisdom and ignore her voice.

> *Lord, may my ears be tuned to hear your voice.*
> *I pray that my steps will not be so rushed that I*
> *will dash past your outstretched hands.*

TODAY'S EVENING READING: Proverbs 1:20–33

DAY 2

Wisdom Verses

"My son, if you receive my words, and treasure my commands
within you ... [and] seek her as silver, and search for her as
for hidden treasures; then you will understand the fear of the
Lord, and find the knowledge of God." —Proverbs 2:1, 4, 5

AN AMAZING FACT: Pirates burying treasure was actually quite rare. The only pirate known to do so was William Kidd, who is believed to have buried some of his wealth on Long Island before traveling to New York. This cache of treasure has never been found.

Every child dreams of finding a hidden treasure. Perhaps that's why so many kid's TV shows, magazines, and even breakfast cereals talk about hidden treasures. There is something tantalizing about the picture of an old wooden chest spilling over with gold and jewels.

Most buried treasure stories in history depict a lone pirate who survives a battle in which all his partners in crime are killed. He somehow preserves a map showing where the hidden treasure can be found. Often, he cannot return to claim the chest of gold and so, while on his deathbed, he passes the information to a friend. This person then tries in vain to find the riches and so must also pass along the secret chart. And so it continues ...

It is the persistence and effort of treasure hunters that Solomon draws to our attention. Wisdom is "more precious than rubies, and all the things you may desire cannot compare with her" (Proverbs 3:15).

In our search for wisdom, we cannot expect it to fall into our laps. We must earnestly hunt for the secret source and do all we can to obtain it. Jesus uses the same idea when describing the kingdom of heaven: "The kingdom of heaven is like treasure hidden in a field, which a man found and hid; and for joy over it he goes and sells all that he has and buys that field" (Matthew 13:44).

God seeks to reward the diligent person who pursues heaven's wisdom. It begins by searching your Bible. In the Book of books, we find Jesus—who reveals to us a true picture of God. Paul explains that in Christ "are hidden all the treasures of wisdom and knowledge" (Colossians 2:3).

While many fables have been written about finding buried treasure, there is a genuine experience we may have when seeking for heavenly wisdom. God promises to reward the earnest at heart. When we are passionate about finding a deeper knowledge of God, we will not reluctantly pass along useless maps. Our dreams will come true. We will find heaven's greatest treasure.

> *Dear Jesus, I want to seek for you with more passion*
> *than I would for hidden treasure. Please reward my*
> *earnest efforts to find you as I study Your Word.*

TODAY'S MORNING READING: Proverbs 2:1–9

DAY 2

Wisdom Verses

"When wisdom enters your heart, and knowledge is
pleasant to your soul, discretion will preserve you;
understanding will keep you." —Proverbs 2:10, 11

AN AMAZING FACT: The most unsuccessful flavor of Life Savers candy was called Malt-O-Milk. Introduced in 1920, it was poorly received by the public and dropped after a couple years.

At some time in your life, you have probably sampled the small circular candy called "Life Savers." The little ring-shaped mints and fruit-flavored candies come in a roll wrapped in aluminum foil. Clarence Crane created them in 1912 as a "summer candy" that wouldn't melt like chocolate. Their name comes from their similarity in shape to lifebuoys, which are used for saving people who fall overboard from boats.

Lifesavers have been around long before 1912—I mean the type used to rescue people from drowning. Some believe the "kisby ring" was first invented by Thomas Kisbee (1792–1877), a British naval officer. Today, many lifebuoys actually have saltwater activators that cause a light to come on inside the buoy, making night rescues easier.

The apostle Paul might have appreciated such a lifesaver during a shipwreck he experienced. While being taken on a ship to Rome as a prisoner, he warned the ship's crew against sailing out of a certain harbor during the storm season and risking the ship and passengers. His wise counsel was ignored—and all on board would have been lost, except for Paul's prayerful intercession. An angel told Paul everyone would be spared but that the ship would be wrecked. As predicted, the ship ran aground and broke into pieces. Passengers soon began to jump overboard and cling to boards and floating cargo. Perhaps this is the closest reference in Scripture to lifesavers!

Our proverb this evening depicts wisdom as a lifesaver that will preserve us through the storms of life. It also tells us that discretion will keep us safe. Knowledge that comes from God helps us to make responsible decisions. Like a good lifebuoy, we can depend on the truth we find in Scripture to protect us from making foolish choices. Clinging to worldly philosophy will only sink us. But like the words of the angel to Paul, wisdom and obedience will give us heavenly buoyancy.

If you are weighed down because you are trying to make an important decision, seek the wisdom of Scripture. Study your Bible for answers. Use your concordance and follow the truths you uncover. Like a lifesaver, God's wisdom will float your life.

> *Dear God, today I place all my choices into your*
> *hands. I ask for your divine wisdom to guide all my*
> *decisions today. May Jesus be my lifesaver!*

TODAY'S EVENING READING: Proverbs 2:10–22

DAY 3

Wisdom Verses

"Do not be wise in your own eyes; fear the Lord and depart from evil. It will be health to your flesh, and strength to your bones." —Proverbs 3:7, 8

AN AMAZING FACT: Everyone has a blind spot in their field of vision because of how nerve fibers pass through the retina and out of the eye. The octopus has no blind spot since the nerve fibers pass behind the retinas of their eyes.

The third chapter of Proverbs lists six commands for us to follow. It also gives us reasons for obeying these instructions. The fourth exhortation in our text for this morning starts with, "Do not be wise in your own eyes." This same directive can be found in several places in Proverbs, most often in reference to fools (Proverbs 12:15; 26:5, 12). What does it mean to be wise in your own eyes?

Those who are wise in their own eyes have a spiritual blind spot. They can be arrogant and have an inflated estimation of their own opinions. Such people are proud, overconfident, and closed to input from others. Solomon's admonition really builds on what comes before in verse 5—"Trust in the Lord." In other words, don't trust in your own wisdom. Acknowledge God in everything you do and He will bless you. Our text promises health and strength when we seek the Lord's ways.

Saul, the first king of Israel, is a prime example of someone who was wise in his own eyes. His position as leader of God's people went to his head. He began to believe that his opinions were always right …

and woe to anyone who would dare cross him! This is why he tried to kill David.

When the Lord instructed Saul to utterly destroy the Amalekites, the arrogant king did not follow God's command. When Samuel confronted the king for disobeying, he insisted he had not transgressed the order. Saul thought so much of himself that he became blind to his own sins—and he ultimately fell on his own sword.

The end result of being wise in our own eyes leads us to separate ourselves from God and, therefore, to self-destruction. When we are independent of the Lord, it ends in detachment from the One who gives life. Because of his blind spots, Saul died tragically. We do not need to follow the same path. Humbly heed God's commands "for length of days and long life and peace they will add to you."

Dear Lord, thank you for your commands. Help me see clearly where I diverge from them. Today I commit to obey your Word and receive the blessings of acknowledging you in all my choices.

TODAY'S MORNING READING: Proverbs 3:1–18

DAY 3

Wisdom Verse

"When you lie down, you will not be afraid; yes, you will lie down and your sleep will be sweet." —Proverbs 3:24

AN AMAZING FACT: It can be difficult to determine if someone is actually awake by mere surface appearances. Many people can take a catnap with their eyes wide open and not even know it!

id you know that the first recorded instance of sleep in history is when God "anesthetized" Adam? Actually, it was a very creative sleep: When Adam awoke he was refreshed, revived ... and married! A whole-new life and, ultimately, the future of humanity can be traced back to that first nap.

Sleep is much more than a passive experience for your body. Although we might be resting, our body is engaged in another type of activity, a process that will bring restoration to frazzled organs, nerves, and body tissues. Sleep is a rejuvenating cycle we all need.

Sleep deprivation can actually be damaging to our bodies and minds. For instance, a lack of sleep impairs our immune system.

One of the longest documented records for a human going without sleep, without using stimulants, is held by Randy Gardner. In 1964, the 17-year-old student stayed awake for 264 hours. (That's 11 days!) Randy reported hallucinations, nausea, paranoia, blurred vision, slurred speech, and memory and concentration lapses. Interestingly, even missing one hour of sleep has been shown to increase the likelihood of a traffic accident by eight percent.

There are lots of tips on getting a good night's rest. Here are just a few: First, wake up with the sun. Sunlight helps to increase levels of alertness, enhancing hormones such as serotonin. Next, eat a balanced diet rich in plant-based complex carbohydrates and tryptophan, which is a building block for hormones like melatonin. Make sure to find time for moderate exercise each day, and avoid sleep-depriving substances like alcohol, caffeine, and nicotine.

But one of the greatest roadblocks to good sleep is worry. Studies show that emotional stress can cause poor-quality sleep. According to Proverbs 3, when we seek God's wisdom and knowledge, our lives will be more relaxed. We are not driven by fear or worry. We will discover that seeking to obey the Lord puts our minds at rest and will actually enhance our sleep. Yes, embracing faith in God like a little child is one of the wisest things you can do to rest easier.

Dear Jesus, tonight as I lay down to sleep, I choose to trust my life with you. I place all my worries into your compassionate hands and will rest in your care.

TODAY'S EVENING READING: Proverbs 3:19–35

DAY 4

Wisdom Verses

"When you walk, your steps will not be hindered, and when you run, you will not stumble. Take firm hold of instruction, do not let go; keep her, for she is your life." —Proverbs 4:12, 13

AN AMAZING FACT: The world record for "walking" on one's hands is held by Sarah Chapman of the United Kingdom. She travelled on her hands 16,404 feet in eight hours on June 3, 2002.

The most famous "walk" in history was probably taken by Neil Armstrong on July 21, 1969, after the Apollo 11 lunar module, the Eagle, landed on the moon. Though the original plan was for Armstrong and Aldrin to rest after landing, they were given permission to suit up right away, depressurize the module, and go outside.

I vividly remember sitting in front of the TV and watching it all play out: Armstrong was the first to descend the ladder. As he reached the bottom step, he turned and planted his left foot onto the powdery surface of the moon and then uttered his now famous words, "That's one small step for [a] man, one giant leap for mankind." (There has actually been a long debate whether the "a" was actually spoken by Neil. Without it, the sentence is a contradiction. Later acoustical analysis supposedly reveals he did state this missing word.)

I believe the most famous steps (other than those of Jesus) recorded in Scripture are taken by those who carry the gospel to others. You've probably sung the words to this Bible verse: "How beautiful upon the mountains are the feet of him who brings good news, who proclaims peace, who brings glad tidings of good things, who proclaims salvation, who says to Zion, 'Your God reigns!' " (Isaiah 52:7).

When we share the love of Jesus, God promises to guide and bless our steps. Since the Lord has called us to witness for Him, we are given the assurance of His angels to keep us from stumbling when we walk in His paths. Perhaps today the Lord will lead you to walk over to a cubicle in the office where you work and hand someone a small piece of literature as you say the words, "I thought you'd enjoy this." Or you might bake a loaf of bread or a batch of cookies and visit a neighbor who is discouraged.

Take a famous walk today. Use your feet to make a giant leap ... for the Lord.

Dear Jesus, because you freely walked the bloodstained path to Calvary, you purchased redemption for all mankind. Thank you.

TODAY'S MORNING READING: Proverbs 4:1–13

DAY 4

Wisdom Verses

"But the path of the just is like the shining sun, that shines ever brighter unto the perfect day. The way of the wicked is like darkness; they do not know what makes them stumble." —Proverbs 4:18, 19

AN AMAZING FACT: Cats have a reflective layer behind their retina that reflects light back into the eye, increasing their night vision by seven times compared to humans.

Light intensity is measured in several ways. Two of the most common are in foot-candles (fc) and in lumens (lux). The old English measure of fc, devised when electricity had yet been harnessed, tells you how much light is projected by a candle over an area of one square foot. One fc is equivalent to one lumen.

Our Bible verse for this evening speaks about how the sun shines brighter unto the perfect day. In other words, after the sun first comes up, it grows brighter and brighter outside until it reaches its apex at high noon. Just for fun, I checked to see what that means in terms of lumens. Just before sunrise, light on a clear morning is around 400 lux. On an overcast day at mid-morning, it measures 10,000 to 25,000 lux. In the shade on a clear sunny day, it can be at 20,000 lux. But at noon on a bright day with no clouds, light can actually reach 120,000 lux!

It all reminds me of the story of Joshua fighting the Amorites at Gibeon. While the Israelite army had not finished destroying the enemy, Joshua said, " 'Sun, stand still over Gibeon; and Moon, in the Valley of Aijalon.' So the sun stood still, and the moon stopped, till the people had revenge upon their enemies. ... So the sun stood still in the midst of heaven, and did not hasten to go down for about a whole day" (Joshua 10:12, 13).

When Joshua needed light to do God's work, the Lord blessed him with the brightest of light. It was a perfect day because Joshua looked to Jehovah for help. On the other hand, people who turn from the Savior walk in darkness. Jesus said, "I am the light of the world. He who follows Me shall not walk in darkness, but have the light of life" (John 8:12). But conversely, when the blind follow the blind, they will stumble. As we keep seeking to follow the Lord, our pathway will grow brighter and brighter.

Lord, may I always walk in your light. I turn
my steps into your pathways of truth.

TODAY'S EVENING READING: Proverbs 4:14–27

DAY 5

Wisdom Verses

"My son, pay attention to my wisdom; lend your ear to my understanding, that you may preserve discretion, and your lips may keep knowledge. For the lips of an immoral woman drip honey, and her mouth is smoother than oil; but in the end she is bitter as wormwood." —Proverbs 5:1–4

AN AMAZING FACT: Humans have about 10,000 taste buds on their tongues, yet insects have the most highly developed sense of taste— using their feet and antennae.

Have you ever taken a bite of some food and suddenly tasted something bitter? (At one potluck, I put some peanut butter on my desert only to discover it was actually vegan cheese spread. Not pretty!) Your first response is to spit it out. Of the five senses of the tongue, bitterness is the most sensitive at picking up something that tastes disagreeable. Perhaps that was God's intention, as many toxic plants have naturally bitter compounds.

The taste threshold of bitterness is measured in relationship to quinine, which is given a reference index of 1. In 1958, scientists discovered a chemical called denatonium, the bitterest substance ever found. It has a threshold of 1,000! This aversive agent is added to poisonous matter to prevent people from accidentally swallowing something that might harm them.

Researchers have also discovered a couple of substances that are extremely bitter to some people but are virtually tasteless to others. Evidently, the genes of some people make them "supertasters" when it comes to identifying certain bitter compounds.

Solomon gives strong medicine to his son in Proverbs 5, urging him to shun immorality at all costs. He speaks from personal experience. It's odd that the wisest man who ever lived made some of the most foolish choices in the area of lust. To all men he warns that what might seem sweet in the beginning ends up being bitter in the end.

He illustrates the remorse and disastrous consequences of breaking the seventh commandment with a perennial plant that grows in the temperate parts of Northern Africa called *artemesia*. The shrub was used as an ingredient in flavoring some alcoholic drinks and in some spices, but the strong bitter juice of the plant is unfit to eat in your typical lunch salad.

God wants us to be supertasters at sensing the poisonous temptations of Satan. Through Solomon's example, the Lord calls to us to "pay attention!" We can learn from Solomon's experiences and be saved from a taste of bitter grief.

Lord, I make a promise to keep my eyes on you today and to keep my thoughts pure. I choose to turn from every polluted pathway.

TODAY'S MORNING READING: Proverbs 5:1–14

DAY 5

Wisdom Verses

"For the ways of man are before the eyes of the LORD, and He ponders all his paths. His own iniquities entrap the wicked man, and he is caught in the cords of his sin." —Proverbs 5:21, 22

AN AMAZING FACT: The Venus flytrap has a special mechanism to prevent it from unnecessarily closing. Its mouth shuts only if an insect triggers a second primary hair within 20 seconds of the first contact.

I'm always amused to read stories of bungled robberies. For example, a woman once attempted to rob a bank in Austria using a stink bomb as her weapon. When she approached the cashier, she told him she had explosives in the box. Then she banged the box down on the counter—accidentally triggering the device! As the nasty smell filled the air, the woman ran out of the building with bank staff quickly following. The police had no problem catching the would-be robber.

It reminds me of the story of the botched plans to capture Elisha the prophet. Every time the king of Syria planned an attack, Elisha would warn the king of Israel and say, "Beware that you do not pass this place, for the Syrians are coming down there" (2 Kings 6:9). It happened so many times that the enemy king became frustrated and accused his servants of treachery—asking them, "Will you not show me which of us is for the king of Israel?" (v. 11).

What they told the king next illustrates our Bible verse for this evening: "And one of his servants said, 'None, my lord, O king; but Elisha, the prophet who is in Israel, tells the king of Israel the words that you speak in your bedroom' " (v. 12). What followed was a fruitless attempt to catch Elisha. When the Syrian king sent an army to surround Dothan, Elisha's servant saw them and was afraid. But God opened the eyes of this fearful man, and he saw the mountains full of horses and chariots of fire.

When the Syrian army marched toward the city, Elisha prayed that the Lord would blind the whole army. The army sent to capture Elisha was captured by Elisha! The prophet then peacefully led the enemy forces to Samaria and into the hands of the king of Israel. Amazingly, instead of being destroyed, the invaders were fed and released. The raiders learned their lesson and "came no more into the land of Israel" (v. 23).

We, too, should remember that the eyes of the Lord see all our actions. We cannot hide anything from God. And when we try to trap others, we might get caught in our own trap.

Father in heaven, you see all, you hear all, you know all. There is nothing hidden from your sight. May all of my choices honor you.

<small>TODAY'S EVENING READING:</small> Proverbs 5:15–23

DAY 6

Wisdom Verses

"How long will you slumber, O sluggard? When will you rise from your sleep? A little sleep, a little slumber, a little folding of the hands to sleep—so shall your poverty come on you like a prowler, and your need like an armed man." —Proverbs 6:9–11

AN AMAZING FACT: An adult bedbug can survive up to one year without feeding.

Sleeping at the wrong time can have detrimental consequences. Many of us have found ourselves nearly nodding off while driving a car after many hours. Airline pilots are required by law to limit how much time they fly between regular sleep. Our ability to make sharp decisions declines when we don't have enough shut-eye.

But our Bible verse for this morning is not about getting enough sleep, but about getting too much sleep and becoming indolent and lazy. Can you picture a sluggard? (This is not the same as a slugger, which is a hard-hitting batter in baseball.) It's that lazy someone who always sleeps in. You can almost see a father calling to his teenager, "When are you ever going to get up and work?" The answer is almost always, "In a little while ... in a little while."

Of course, we know the results of being slothful. How many individuals might improve their situation with a good work ethic, if they pushed themselves a little bit more? Sometimes when I visit people in my pastoral work and listen to their tales of woe, I sense that it has become more comfortable for some to sit and watch TV than to unfold their hands, get up, and put on a pair of work gloves.

But there is also a poverty that is worse than being low on cash. Paul writes, "In Him we have redemption through His blood, the forgiveness of sins, according to the riches of His grace which He made to abound toward us" (Ephesians 1:7, 8). The wealth in this passage does not simply fall into our hands. We must earnestly reach for it and put forth earnest effort.

God does not want us to live apathetic lives. Solomon challenges all of us to "go to the ant, you sluggard! Consider her ways and be wise, which having no captain, oversee or ruler, provides her supplies in the summer, and gathers her food in the harvest" (Proverbs 6:6–8). Even the smallest of God's creatures can show us how to live industriously.

Dear Lord, today I determine to live fully for you. Guide my plans and direct my paths. May all of my work honor you.

TODAY'S MORNING READING: Proverbs 6:1–19

DAY 6

Wisdom Verses

"Can a man take fire to his bosom, and his clothes not be burned? Can one walk on hot coals, and his feet not be seared? So is he who goes in to his neighbor's wife; whoever touches her shall not be innocent." —Proverbs 6:27–29

AN AMAZING FACT: You have about 17,000 tactile receptors on your hands, with around 100 on each fingertip.

God created us with thousands of sensory receptors in our skin that tell us about the world around us. Some are sensitive to pressure and pain, hot and cold, and even vibration. The numbers and locations of these receptors are not all the same. There are also far more pain receptors in the body than cold receptors. Moreover, our sense of touch is greater in places like our fingertips and far less in the middle of our back.

There are lots of emotions we can communicate with touch—love, anger, joy, sadness, peace, irritability, etc. We don't need words to tell someone to get out of the way or that we are happy to see them. There is power in touch. We can actually reduce our loved one's blood pressure when we reach out and give him or her a friendly hug or a squeeze of the hand.

But not all touch is appropriate. When Potiphar's wife tried to seduce Joseph into committing adultery, Joseph said, "How then can I do this great wickedness, and sin against God?" (Genesis 39:9). She was persistent, and one day, when nobody was around, grabbed on to Joseph.

Notice how this young man of God responded to this wrong touch: "But he left his garment in her hand, and fled and ran outside" (v. 12).

Several times in the book of Proverbs, Solomon warns his son about the perils of adultery. He knew the pitfalls because the king of Israel fell prey to the sin of fornication. "King Solomon loved many foreign women ... from the nations of whom the LORD had said to the children of Israel, 'You shall not intermarry with them, nor they with you. Surely they will turn away your hearts after other gods.' Solomon clung to these in love" (1 Kings 11:1, 2).

Joseph did not cling to the touch of Potiphar's wife ... he ran. His example is the one we should follow. Solomon took fire into his bosom, and it scorched his life and scarred his children. Let's follow the path of Joseph and stay pure.

> *Dear Jesus, I commit all of my thoughts and*
> *actions to you. I choose to never touch others*
> *inappropriately. I will keep myself pure and true.*

TODAY'S EVENING READING: Proverbs 6:20–35

DAY 7

Wisdom Verses

"My son, keep my words, and treasure my commands
within you. Keep my commands and live, and my law
as the apple of your eye." —Proverbs 7:1, 2

AN AMAZING FACT: Two brown-eyed parents can have a blue-eyed baby—but two blue-eyed parents cannot have a baby with brown eyes.

The human eye is one of the most fascinating and complex organs of the body. It is one of the many features of creation that has baffled evolutionists because of the intricate and interdependent way in which it functions. The dark hole in the middle of our eye is called the pupil. It is black because light entering inside is absorbed. Muscles surrounding the pupil can expand and contract to adjust the size of the hole, permitting more or less light to enter the eye—much like a camera aperture.

Proverbs 7 is another call to purity by Solomon and describes keeping God's law as the "apple of your eye." What does this mean? Generally, it speaks of someone (or something) that you cherish above all else. The original Hebrew idiom behind this phrase is literally translated "little man of the eye." Some believe that it is a reference to the reflection you can see of yourself in someone else's pupils. Others suggest "apple" was simply the translator's creative description for what is simply "the dark spot" of the eye.

Whatever the exact origin of the phrase, what is clear to Solomon is that if we are to live a pure and holy life, then God's law must be central in our thinking. When we allow impure thoughts and pictures to enter our pupils, it pollutes our thoughts. Solomon's father, King David, allowed this to happen when looking upon Bathsheba. Instead of turning his eyes away, he permitted what he saw to set aside God's law. It clouded his vision and led him into sin and a horrific train wreck of consequences.

When we keep God's law as the apple of our eye, we meditate on His precepts and hold the commandments up before us. We not only read them, we also seek to live by them. The reflection of the law in our eyes can be seen by others. Jesus said, "The lamp of the body is the eye. If therefore your eye is good, your whole body will be full of light" (Matthew 6:22). Focus on the beauty of God's law today and it will enlighten your eyes (Psalm 19:8).

> *Dear Lord, open my eyes that I may see the glimpses*
> *of truth you have for me. Place in my hand the*
> *wonderful key that shall unclasp and set me free.*

TODAY'S MORNING READING: Proverbs 7:1–12

DAY 7

Wisdom Verses

"With her enticing speech she caused him to yield, with her flattering lips she seduced him. Immediately he went after her, as an ox goes to the slaughter." —Proverbs 7:21, 22

AN AMAZING FACT: In the United States, about nine billion animals are slaughtered annually for food. Each year Americans consume more than 13.6 million tons of beef.

Slaughterhouses are not popular with the public. Though most people enjoy eating the end product, there is an aversion to the gruesome process of killing animals. In many places local laws actually specify where meat packing plants can and can't be located. Animal welfare groups criticize the often callous methods of transporting, preparing, herding, and killing animals.

It is really unpleasant to think about the procedure. Cattle are driven in trucks or by rail hundreds of miles from a ranch or feedlot, typically in crowded conditions. Not all make it to the slaughterhouse alive. Then they are shuttled through narrow corrals and brought into holding pens where they are "incapacitated." I didn't think much about this stuff when I ran a meat sales business in my VW many years back, but let's just say that after hanging the animal upside down and draining out most of the blood, butchers begin to do their grisly work.

Does this process disgust you? I won't explain the details of turning a cow into "food" for your local burger shop. Most of my readers are thinking, "Stop talking about this! What's the value in even thinking about it?" Let me tell you. ... This is the analogy that Solomon uses to describe the fate of foolish young (or old) men, (this would apply to women as well), who are seduced into breaking God's commandment on adultery. What seems like a flower-strewn pathway ends up being the road to hell.

Solomon says of this foolish man that he "immediately" goes after her. In other words, he is controlled by his carnal nature and passions, not his rational brain. Like a bird flying into a net, "He did not know it would cost his life" (v. 23). Sin confuses us into thinking about the moment and not the true end-result. No wonder the wise man says, "Do not stray into her paths; for she has cast down many wounded, and all who were slain by her were strong men. Her house is the way to hell, descending to the chambers of death" (vv. 25-27). It's a one-way tunnel you don't ever want to enter.

> *Lord, give me a clear vision for keeping my mind*
> *and heart always before you. May I never wander*
> *close to Satan's deadly slaughterhouse.*

TODAY'S EVENING READING: Proverbs 7:13–27

DAY 8

Wisdom Verses

*"All the words of my mouth are with righteousness; nothing crooked
or perverse is in them. They are all plain to him who understands,
and right to those who find knowledge." —Proverbs 8:8, 9*

AN AMAZING FACT: With eight tight hairpin turns down a 27 percent grade, Lombard Street in San Francisco has been dubbed the most crooked street in the world.

Maybe you've driven down the red-bricked Lombard Street when touring the City by the Bay. It's kind of fun to travel down the one-block section famous for it corkscrew turns. Carl Henry, a property owner, first suggested adding switchbacks to deal with the quarter mile section that was much too steep for most automobiles at the time. That happened in 1922. Even walking up this hill is tough on most people.

Our text for this morning contrasts righteous speech with talk that is perverse or "crooked." The King James uses the word "froward," which means to be habitually disposed to disobedience. Good speech is honest and straightforward. People whose mouths speak unrighteous words are perverse. What they say is winding and shaped more like a slithering snake. That matches Satan, whom Jesus calls the father of lies (John 8:44). His first conversation with Eve was definitely crooked!

This reminds me of the time Jehoshaphat, king of Judah, went to visit Ahab, king of Israel, to discuss attacking Ramoth Gilead. When Ahab called upon 400 prophets to give him advice, they all said, "Go up, for the LORD will deliver it into the hand of the king" (1 Kings 22:6). But

Jehoshaphat said, "Is there not still a prophet of the LORD here, that we may inquire of Him" (v. 7). Ahab said there was one man, Micaiah, but he hated listening to him because this prophet spoke the truth.

Straight talk has never been popular. It put Jeremiah in prison and cost John the Baptist his head. On multiple occasions, the apostle Paul was beaten for speaking the truth. And most of all, honesty led Jesus to be nailed to a cross for our sins. All Christ's words were true.

The reason a river is crooked is because it follows the path of least resistance. This is why some lives are also crooked. The path of the righteous might not always be easy, but it is straight. The way to heaven is through Jesus. When we speak with unswerving faith in the Lord, we will reach our destination—heaven!

Today, Lord, I choose to speak the truth in love. I commit to walk on the straight pathway to heaven. I will utter no perverse words.

TODAY'S MORNING READING: Proverbs 8:1–21

DAY 8

E V E N I N G

Wisdom Verses

"The LORD possessed me at the beginning of His way, before His works of old. I have been established from everlasting, from the beginning, before there was ever an earth." —Proverbs 8:22, 23

AN AMAZING FACT: One of the oldest mechanical clocks in the world is the Salisbury Cathedral clock in England—a large, iron-framed timepiece dating from around 1386.

One of the interesting features of the Salisbury Cathedral clock is that it doesn't have a dial with numbers to indicate time. It was a "single strike" clock, striking a bell on the hour—two strikes for 2 o'clock, five strikes for 5 o'clock, etc. It was powered by two large stone weights and needed to be wound twice a day. Over the years the clock was modified, and, at the end of the 17th century, a pendulum and anchor was added to its operation.

There's actually a debate as to whether the Salisbury Cathedral clock is the oldest mechanical clock in the world. There are several 14th century clocks, some destroyed, some lost, and some substantially modified. When a new clock was placed in the Salisbury Cathedral in 1884, the old one was set aside. Then in 1928, T.R. Robinson, an horological enthusiast, discovered the clock and believed it to be the timepiece mentioned in records as dating to 1386.

Our text for this evening is also debated among theologians as to the origins of Jesus. Some believe the reference in this verse to Christ means He must have been created at some point in time. Because of the many references in the Bible to Jesus being divine (Hebrews 1:5–9) and existing from everlasting times (John 1:1; John 8:58; Isaiah 9:6; 1 Timothy 6:15, 16, etc.), I look at the meaning of this passage through the whole of Scripture.

There is a clear parallel to wisdom and Jesus in this text. A better word for "possessed" is "begot me," meaning "to establish." In other words, Christ was installed or designated in the godhead as the One who would be directly involved in the creation of our world. Verse 22 says that wisdom (who we may understand as Jesus) was "before His works of old." Hebrews 1:2 supports this view.

We may be confident, through the testimony of Scripture, that Christ existed before all time. Before clocks kept track of hours and days, before books recorded history, and before archaeologists dug up the most ancient of artifacts, Jesus existed. He is the divine Son of God from all eternity.

Dear Jesus, I believe in you as my divine Creator.
I trust in you as my living Savior. In you is life, and
I joyfully and humbly receive your gift of salvation.

TODAY'S EVENING READING: Proverbs 8:22–36

DAY 9

Wisdom Verse

*"Wisdom has built her house, she has hewn
out her seven pillars." —Proverbs 9:1*

AN AMAZING FACT: Though the Winchester Mystery House is one of the most popular mansions in California, the Victorian home completely lacks a master building plan.

Sarah Winchester just had to move from Connecticut. According to a medium that she consulted after her husband's death, the supposed spirits of all the dead people killed by guns manufactured by her husband's famous company would haunt her unless she kept building a house. People say her deceased husband also communicated that she would *not* die if she continued construction on a home. So, in 1884, she moved west to San Jose and hired carpenters to begin working day and night.

In order to "confuse the spirits" and prevent them from settling into the home (which supposedly happened anyway since it was apparently "haunted"), Sarah built many strange features into her mansion. You can find doors that lead nowhere and windows that look into other parts of the house. Sarah inherited $20.5 million when her husband passed away. Besides that, her income from part ownership in the Winchester Repeating Arms Company gave her about $1,000 a day (about $30,000 a day in today's value). Though she kept her workers busy building 24 hours a day, seven days a week, for 36 years, Sarah died on September 5, 1922. The next day all construction ceased.

On the other hand, one of the most beautiful homes built in Bible times had a perfect plan. God's sanctuary design was originally communicated to Moses. Later, when David intended to construct a permanent location for the Lord's house, his son, King Solomon, erected the "First Temple" in Jerusalem. It was so carefully crafted that materials were prepared offsite and then brought to the location and reverently placed.

Jesus promised that He would build heavenly mansions for each of us, but the preparation that we need to make before receiving those homes is to receive Christ into our hearts. In other words, God's temple would be built within us and we would house the Holy Spirit. Paul writes, "Do you not know that your body is the temple of the Holy Spirit who is in you, whom you have from God, and you are not your own?" (1 Corinthians 6:19).

In Hebrew, seven is *shevah*, which comes from the root word *savah*, meaning to be full or satisfied. Because it means full and satisfied, it is, therefore, the number of spiritual perfection. God's wisdom helps us build the perfect home. Solomon is telling us that wisdom has made a house without flaw. The Bible is our blueprint. When we take the knowledge of the Scriptures into our minds, we will live forever.

Dear Jesus, just as you worked as a master craftsman in a
carpenter's shop, please build your likeness into my heart today.

TODAY'S MORNING READING: Proverbs 9:1–9

DAY 9

Wisdom Verses

"'Stolen water is sweet, and bread eaten in secret is pleasant.'
But he does not know that the dead are there, that her
guests are in the depths of hell." —Proverbs 9:17, 18

AN AMAZING FACT: The number of unmarried couples living together has risen in the United States from 439,000 in 1960 to 5,500,000 in the year 2000—an increase of 1,153 percent.

In Proverbs 9 we see again that wisdom is personified as a woman. But in the last half we see another woman called "folly." She also sits in the highest places in the city, calling out to the masses to come to her house. This foolish woman is described as loud, simple, and knows nothing (v. 13). Like the immoral woman in Proverbs 7, she makes promises that are empty and lead to death.

I am distressed that the call of this foolish woman is making an impact in the United States. According to a 2013 Gallup Poll, the number of people who said gay and lesbian relationships were okay has moved from 40 percent 12 years ago to almost 60 percent today. About 45 percent of Americans felt having a baby outside of marriage was morally acceptable in 2001. Today it has jumped up to 60 percent.

Stolen water is not sweet; it is poison. Bread eaten in secret is not pleasant; it will destroy you. Too many are seduced by the false allure of immoral living and believe they can avoid negative consequences. It is a sad commentary to see so many broken marriages. There has been a huge increase in sexually transmitted diseases as well. People scarcely react to news of adultery, fornication, prostitution, and lewd behavior.

God looks with disgust on the pollution that has been poured all over society. We can see this by looking at the judgments against Israel when they camped at the Jordan. During Moses' final days, Midianite women came into camp and seduced the men of Israel to participate in vulgar acts of idolatrous worship. "If anyone defiles the temple of God, God will destroy him. For the temple of God is holy, which temple you are" (1 Corinthians 3:17).

This reminds me of Samson allowing himself to be caressed to sleep on the lethal lap of Delilah. This man chosen by God became careless in following wise counsel. By feasting on the secret bread and stolen waters, Samson lost his strength and then his eyes.

The morally blind person "does not know that the dead are there, that her guests are in the depths of hell" (v. 18). Wisdom is not blind. "For by me your days will be multiplied, and years of life will be added to you" (v. 11). When foolishness calls to you, turn away. Follow in the path of life.

Lord, every day I want to eat the bread of life. I turn my heart to Jesus, the only water that will quench my deepest thirst.

TODAY'S EVENING READING: Proverbs 9:10–18

Wisdom Verse

"The mouth of the righteous is a well of life, but violence covers the mouth of the wicked." —Proverbs 10:11

AN AMAZING FACT: About 75 percent of Americans are chronically dehydrated. Lack of water is the number one trigger of daytime fatigue.

Many people don't realize how much their body needs water. The thirst mechanism in 37 percent of Americans is so weak that it is often mistaken for hunger. Even if you are mildly dehydrated, it can slow down your metabolism by as much as three percent.

Drinking enough water can help you with a host of problems. The University of Washington studied dieters and discovered that drinking only one glass of water would shut down midnight hunger pangs in 100 percent of people. Joint pain in 80 percent of sufferers can be reduced by consuming 8 to 10 glasses of water per day. And only five glasses of water per day would decrease the risk of colon cancer by 45 percent.

What caught my attention in water research was that just a two-percent drop in body water can contribute to fuzzy short-term memory, make it difficult to do simple math, and cause trouble focusing on reading a book or looking at a computer screen. Perhaps even our Bible study time would improve if we drank enough water!

When Jesus spoke to the Samaritan woman at the well about water, He drew her attention to Himself as the source of living water. "Whoever drinks of the water that I shall give him will never thirst. But the water that I shall give him will become in him a fountain of water springing up into everlasting life" (John 4:14). It's kind of like an artesian well that feeds from a higher altitude, causing pressure to naturally force the water to spring up.

The Bible verse for this morning describes the righteous as speaking words that are a source of life. We also can be like Jesus and talk with others about God. We can share our faith and point people to Christ, the Fountain of Living Water, who will never leave them feeling spiritually dehydrated. The purest water from Jesus comes from the Bible. When we allow the Lord to guide us, we will "be like a watered garden, and like a spring of water, whose waters do not fail" (Isaiah 58:11).

> *"Come thou Fount of every blessing, tune my heart to sing thy grace; streams of mercy, never ceasing, call for songs of loudest praise."*

TODAY'S MORNING READING: Proverbs 10:1–15

DAY 10

Wisdom Verses

"In the multitude of words sin is not lacking, but he who restrains his lips is wise. The tongue of the righteous is choice silver; the heart of the wicked is worth little." —Proverbs 10:19, 20

AN AMAZING FACT: The largest tongue in the world is found in the blue whale. Its tongue is the size of an elephant and weighs 5,400 pounds.

You might think that your tongue is a small organ and not extremely important, but without it you could not eat, talk, spit, swallow, or even kiss! Scientists have even determined that the tongue is, pound for pound, the strongest muscle in your body even though it is the only muscle that is attached at only one end.

The human tongue has been listed in world records as well. The longest human tongue on record is 3.86 inches from tip to the back. Contrary to "old wives' tales," women have shorter tongues than men. Thomas Blackstone holds the record for having the strongest tongue; he actually lifted a 24-pound, 3-ounce weight with his tongue.

According to the World Record Academy, Fran Capo is the world's fastest talking female. She was clocked at 603 words in 54 seconds. That comes to 11 words a second! She first broke the world record on the *Larry King Live* show in 1986 when she spoke 585 words per minute. Before you think I'm biased about women talking, let me add that Steve Woodmore from England was clocked at 637 words per minute!

Solomon has something to say about lots of words. Our text this evening reminds us that people who talk a lot can be inclined to say things they regret. When our tongues move faster than our brains, we're in for trouble. The Bible often warns us to watch what we say. James writes,

> "Look also at ships: although they are so large and are driven by fierce winds, they are turned by a very small rudder wherever the pilot desires. Even so the tongue is a little member and boasts great things. See how great a forest a little fire kindles! And the tongue is a fire, a world of iniquity. The tongue is so set among our members that it defiles the whole body, and sets on fire the course of nature; and it is set on fire by hell" (James 3:4–6).

The proverb encourages us that he "who restrains his lips is wise." Guard your tongue. It is not the number of words you speak that demonstrates your intelligence; it is the care with which you choose them.

Lord, I pray that my words will be like choice silver,
valuable in honoring you and uplifting others.

TODAY'S EVENING READING: Proverbs 10:16–32

45

DAY 11

Wisdom Verse

"Where there is no counsel, the people fall; but in the
multitude of counselors there is safety." —Proverbs 11:14

AN AMAZING FACT: The people of the United States spend about
$115 billion on mental health treatment each year, with 27 percent of
that going toward prescription drugs.

O f course, our text for this morning is not speaking about paid
professional counselors. While I believe that therapy has a
place and that there are times when a godly counselor can help
a person work through issues, the passage above isn't about trained
specialists. (I am concerned about the speed with which people seek help
in medications, however. God has given us excellent natural remedies
that should not be overlooked.)

The Hebrew word for "counsel" in this passage grows out of the
word used for the ropes that were pulled to change the direction of a
ship at sea. The picture is one of guidance and new direction. When a
person, or group of people, refuses to listen to advice, he might find
himself shipwrecked. That's often true with married couples. One of the
determining factors for a successful marriage is a husband who is open
to suggestions. When a man is adamant about his viewpoints and will
not consider his wife's perspective, it's a sure sign that their relationship
will crumble.

Not all counsel is good. A classic example of two different types of
counsel in the Bible is found in the story of Solomon's son, Rehoboam.

When his father died, the people complained about heavy taxes to their new king. He sent them away for three days before giving them a response.

Rehoboam first consulted with his father's experienced counselors. They advised him to back off and treat the people more kindly. But he disliked their counsel and instead asked young men whom he had grown up with for advice. They suggested the young king show the people he was boss. They recommended he threatened to increase their taxes and treat them even more harshly. He accepted this foolish advice and subsequently lost half of the kingdom.

Wise counsel can save us from a lot of heartache, not only in our homes, but also in our churches and businesses. When skillful advice is lacking, people can be led into reckless pathways of destruction. But when we are open to listen to wisdom from gifted and experienced people, when there is open discussion tempered by humility, we will find ourselves in safer places.

Father in heaven, when you speak to me today
through your Word or through godly people, may I
humbly listen and grow to value godly advice.

TODAY'S MORNING READING: Proverbs 11:1–15

DAY 11

Wisdom Verse

*"The fruit of the righteous is a tree of life, and he
who wins souls is wise." —Proverbs 11:30*

AN AMAZING FACT: One tree can absorb as much carbon dioxide in a year as an automobile creates driving 26,000 miles.

The longest living organism on our planet is the tree. It's also one of the greatest natural resources we have. Trees help to keep our air clean. Just one tree can produce about 260 pounds of clean oxygen per year. Over the course of its life, a tree can absorb about one ton of carbon dioxide. An acre of trees can remove 2.6 tons of carbon dioxide in a year.

Trees benefit us in many other ways. If they are well-maintained, trees can increase our property value and the soil quality. Properly placed trees around buildings can reduce air conditioning needs by 30 percent. Wind buffering provided by trees can also lower our heating bills in the winter. Of course, I could talk about lumber and paper products we get from trees, along with fruit to feed our families.

Our text for this evening says, "The fruit of the righteous is a tree of life" (Proverbs 11:30). People who live according to the wisdom and knowledge of God are a nurturing blessing to others. Their conduct and words bring life, healing, and encouragement to those around them. Perhaps you've been next to someone who "drains" you—someone who is usually focused on himself and only wants to get from others.

On the other hand, some folks seem to inspire you when you are in their company. Their presence lifts you and gives you energy. Much like the tree of life in the garden of Eden, people who live according to God's laws are a gift of life to those close by. Jesus was like this. When men, women, and children were close to Christ, they were transformed. And others could tell.

When Peter and John were arrested for preaching about Jesus, they were brought before the Sanhedrin and questioned. The disciples spoke so courageously about the Lord that the Bible says of the Jewish rulers, "Now when they saw the boldness of Peter and John, and perceived that they were uneducated and untrained men, they marveled. And they realized that they had been with Jesus" (Acts 4:13).

We win souls by reflecting Jesus to others. The wisest thing we can do is lead others to the cross of Christ, which is the ultimate tree of life.

Dear Lord, may my life be fruitful and give
strength to others. May the hope and peace I
receive from you bless others around me.

TODAY'S EVENING READING: Proverbs 11:16–31

49

DAY 12

Wisdom Verse

*"Whoever loves instruction loves knowledge, but he
who hates correction is stupid." —Proverbs 12:1*

AN AMAZING FACT: The total number of high school dropouts annually in the United States is 3,030,000. The percent of U.S. jobs a high school dropout is *not* eligible for is about 90 percent.

If you read my book *The Richest Caveman*, you know that I attended some pretty interesting schools in my younger years, including two different military academies, a school on board a ship, and one place that threw all rules out the window. This experimental school in Maine believed that kids will learn the things that are important to them. Well, I guess it was true, though most of what I learned was from other students ... and the things I learned weren't very profitable!

I made the reckless decision to drop out of high school at 16 and run away. By the time I was 20, I realized my prospects for success would be very limited, so I earned my GED and went on to college.

Today I always encourage young people to get a good education. High school dropouts are more likely to be unemployed, earn lower wages, be more dependent on government assistance, and to be single parents. Even crime stats show that 30 percent of federal inmates have not completed high school, and 50 percent of convicts on death row have not finished grade 12.

The wise teacher in Proverbs says, "Whoever loves instruction loves knowledge." In other words, if you really want to learn something, you'll go through the discipline of getting it, no matter how difficult. We are shortsighted to think we can learn to play the piano but never practice or get our driver's license but never study for the written exam. We should love instruction because we want to go somewhere and be someone.

Sometimes I hear students say, "I can't wait until I graduate so that I don't have to take any more tests!" I hate to pop their bubbles, but I tell them life will continue to throw many tests at them. Almost every occupation requires an element of training, study, and ongoing assessment to maintain licenses. Many jobs call for continuing education units. The idea of taking tests should not drag you down. Exams and evaluations open doors of opportunity!

God has given us minds to expand and develop. Peter writes, "Grow in the grace and knowledge of our Lord and Savior Jesus Christ" (2 Peter 3:18). Education is a lifelong endeavor for the Christian. We do not stop learning when we graduate from school. We continue seeking to stretch our minds and grasp more of the truths of Scripture and the things God has created.

Lord, help me to learn something new today. You gave me a mind. Help me to use it for your kingdom and your glory.

TODAY'S MORNING READING: Proverbs 12:1–14

DAY 12

Wisdom Verse

"The righteous should choose his friends carefully, for the
way of the wicked leads them astray." —Proverbs 12:26

AN AMAZING FACT: A 2004 Gallup poll indicates that the average
American has nine close friends.

In this same poll, 73 percent of Americans say they are satisfied with the number of friends they have, but 23 percent wish they had a few more friends. It's interesting that the number of friends drops to seven for those in their 30s and 40s, but rises to 12 for those over 65. The researchers also discovered that the more money people made, the fewer friends they had.

In a similar study on friends and churches, Gallup found that people who have friends within their own church could more fully live out their faith than those who tended to have friends outside their church. In other words, if you don't have friends at church, it can actually impede your spiritual growth! Being isolated or having the wrong types of friends can pull you away from God. My father used to say, "If you sleep with dogs, you'll get fleas."

We often think of choosing friends as a thing to do during our teen years. But while it's true that young people can develop new friendships that will last a lifetime, the principle of choosing our friends wisely is for every age. People might move to a new community or attend a new church or begin a new job and have opportunity to forge new relationships. Good friends at any age can be a powerful influence in our lives.

For instance, I'm impressed with the positive peer influence of friends when I read the story of Shadrach, Meshach, and Abed-Nego. It's an example of how the right friends can help you withstand intense peer pressure. King Nebuchadnezzar built a golden image nearly 90-feet tall and commanded all his government officials to come for the dedication. At the king's command, everyone was to bow down and worship the image—or face immediate execution. The three young Hebrews didn't bow down; they stood strong together. As a result, they were thrown into the fiery furnace together ... only to be miraculously rescued by God!

Choose your friends wisely, because they will influence your life. Avoid making close friendships with those who are rejecting God. Watch out for people with hot tempers. "Make no friendship with an angry man, and with a furious man do not go" (Proverbs 22:24). Beware of gossipers. Rather, spend time with those who have high values and stay near people with whom you can be honest. Your choices will impact your final destiny.

> *Dear Father in heaven, please guide my choices in making*
> *friends. May I pick carefully those I spend time with.*
> *Thank you for sending Jesus to be my best friend.*

TODAY'S EVENING READING: Proverbs 12:15–28

53

DAY 13

Wisdom Verse

"There is one who makes himself rich, yet has nothing; and one who makes himself poor, yet has great riches." —Proverbs 13:7

AN AMAZING FACT: More than $13 billion worth of goods are stolen from retailers each year. That amounts to more than $35 million every day.

Shoplifting is a serious problem in the United States. One in 11 people steal goods from stores. That's about 27 million offenders. They take from all types of stores and have no typical profile. Men and women are equally prone to this type of thievery. Approximately 25 percent of shoplifters are kids. About three percent are "professional" in their work, stealing for the purpose of reselling products. But the vast majority of shoplifters are non-professionals.

Why do people shoplift? The professionals often are drug addicts who steal to feed their bad habit. Others are part of larger operations, running illegal businesses. But most people who steal have no other major criminal intent or a desire for financial gain. They are driven by social and personal pressures in their lives. Many get addicted to this evil habit and actually like the excitement of "getting away with it." Called kleptomania, it's almost like a high from taking drugs.

Our text for this morning says, "There is one who makes himself rich" but has nothing. In other words, there are people who hoard wealth or pretend to be wealthy. They want so badly to look good that they will take extreme measures to appear affluent. But it's all emptiness.

It's like the foolish man in Jesus' parable (Luke 12:16–21) who thought by building bigger barns and hoarding his possessions, he would find peace. In reality his life was about to end and he would enter the grave and eternity with nothing.

On the other hand, when the apostles asked Jesus, "See, we have left all and followed You. Therefore what shall we have?" Jesus responded, "Assuredly, I say to you, there is no one who has left house or brothers or sisters or father or mother or wife or children or lands, for My sake and the gospel's, who shall not receive a hundredfold now in this time—houses and brothers and sisters and mothers and children and lands, with persecutions—and in the age to come, eternal life" (Mark 10:27, 29–30).

When we come to Christ and admit our sinfulness and our great need, the Lord gives us the gift of eternal life. It's a blessing that cannot be measured in dollars.

> *Thank you, Lord, for the gift of salvation offered by Jesus.*
> *May I not seek to become rich in the eyes of this world,*
> *but may I become truly rich by receiving your grace.*

TODAY'S MORNING READING: Proverbs 13:1–12

DAY 13

Wisdom Verse

*"He who walks with wise men will be wise, but the companion
of fools will be destroyed." —Proverbs 13:20*

AN AMAZING FACT: The average person will walk about 65,000
miles in his or her lifetime—that's three times around the earth!

Caleb Smith is a dedicated walker. When he moved to the Big
Apple, he was so enamored by the little-known places that he
decided to purchase a map and walk on all the roads, avenues,
and streets on the entire island. He eventually covered about 700 miles.
He was inspired by Thomas Keane, a man who did the same walk in 1954.
Caleb finished his walk on December 19, 2004, the 50th anniversary of
Keane meeting his goal.

I think we underestimate the health benefits of simply walking. For
instance, Duke University Medical Center found that a brisk 30-minute
walk three times a week was just as effective as antidepressant
medication in relieving the symptoms of major depression. A study in
the Archives of Internal Medicine showed that older women who walked
regularly were less likely to develop memory loss. And the Mayo Clinic
uncovered evidence that walking positively affects the levels of certain
mood-enhancing neurotransmitters in the brain.

You don't read about the health benefits of walking in the
Bible. People didn't read books and articles on getting this form of
exercise because their feet were the standard mode of transportation.
Jesus and His disciples didn't take the bus from Jericho to Jerusalem.

They didn't ride the train from Galilee to Bethany. They walked everywhere they went!

What made the walking excursions of the disciples so beneficial was not just the fresh, unpolluted air in Palestine. They walked with Jesus, their Master and Teacher. Christ was the wisest of all people who ever walked the face of the earth, much wiser than even Solomon. It was common for ancient sages to have a group of students to teach. Many of them shared their wisdom with their disciples while walking. As they passed through villages and trekked the countryside, these teachers would point to the things around them as a means of illustrating their wisdom.

We also may walk with Christ. We may walk with the wisest Teacher and, as our proverb this evening states, become wise. The knowledge of Scripture, given to us by the Lord, will lead us to someday walk streets of gold. That's a trek I don't want to miss!

"I am weak, but Thou art strong; Keep me Jesus from all wrong;
I'll be satisfied as long as I walk, dear Lord, close to Thee."

TODAY'S EVENING READING: Proverbs 13:13–25

DAY 14

Wisdom Verse

"Even in laughter the heart may sorrow, and the end
of mirth may be grief." —Proverbs 14:13

AN AMAZING FACT: The world record for someone continuously laughing is held by Belachew Girma from Ethiopia. He laughed without taking a break for three hours and six minutes.

Ethiopia is often not a country filled with lots of laughter and smiles. It has been plagued by drought and poverty. Belachew suffered from his own disasters as well. He was a drug addict and an alcoholic. His life spiraled downward until he was ready to commit suicide. What turned him around was finding a Bible and also a book that encouraged laughter as a form of therapy. Mr. Girma used to laugh while under the influence of drugs. But now his infectious chuckling from joy has so changed his life that he has actually opened Girma's School of Laughter to teach others how to laugh.

Did you know there are websites that teach you how to fake a laugh? First you are supposed to get into the spirit by reading some jokes. Then you practice laughing, whether you feel like it or not. You can cover your mouth, which is supposed to help. And, of course, if you are caught laughing when you don't really mean it, you should just change the subject.

Why do people laugh when they don't really mean it? It's probably because we don't want to hurt other people's feelings. If someone tells a joke and you don't think it's funny, you might laugh just to be polite.

What's sad is how well it works. Many people think they're funny or smart when the truth is that others are simply not honest about what they are thinking.

Not all laughter is healing. Some people who laugh on the outside are not genuinely happy at all. There are shallow and cheap forms of entertainment, jokes that are crude, and gossip that makes fun of others that will cause some people to laugh. But in the end, hearts might still be empty and hurting. The Bible teaches us that there are times for laughter and times for crying (Ecclesiastes 3:4).

Solomon tells us that not all laughter is genuine. Sometimes when we hear other people laugh, we might assume everything is okay, but deep down inside a person might be in distress. Other times people laugh as a way to avoid facing a difficulty in their life. Turning away from certain problems, like an addiction or other sinful habit, will eventually increase our sorrow and grief. Wisdom knows the difference in our laughing.

Dear Lord, thank you for the gift of laughter.
May I bring true joy into the lives of others today.
And help me to recognize hurting hearts around me.

<small>TODAY'S MORNING READING:</small> Proverbs 14:1–19

DAY 14

Wisdom Verses

*"The poor man is hated even by his own neighbor, but the rich
has many friends. He who despises his neighbor sins; but he who
has mercy on the poor, happy is he." —Proverbs 14:20, 21*

AN AMAZING FACT: According to World Bank statistics, the poorest
country in the world is the Democratic Republic of Congo (DRC), with
an annual GDP per capita of only $422.

There are different ways to measure the poverty of a country.
Calculations made by various organizations consider purchasing power, cost of living, inflation rates, and standard of living.
But whether you look at the World Bank, International Monetary Fund,
or Central Intelligence Agency figures, the DRC still comes out rock
bottom. (Not to be confused with the Republic of Congo, the DRC was
known as Zaire until 1997.)

In this impoverished country of 71 million people, where French is
the official language, the Second Congo War, which began in 1998, has
devastated the country. It's a confrontation involving seven foreign
armies and has been noted as the deadliest conflict in the world since
World War II, killing 5.4 million people. I don't even want to describe
the violation of human rights that takes place there, particularly among
women. The United Nations calls the DRC the rape capital of the world.

It's challenging to think about how to help your poor neighbor, but
try to grasp how to help an entire country! Sending money and even
shipments of food to starving people in such places is difficult because of

corruption. The people who are starving might never see a grain of rice because of fraud and dishonesty. Donors have become wary of dropping dollars into extended hands. In the long run, it is more effective to dig wells and to teach agricultural, business, and reading skills.

Solomon's proverb this evening begins with what most people think is true for all the wrong reasons: "The poor man is hated even by his own neighbor, but the rich has many friends" (Proverbs 14:20). There are many people who are poor by this world's standards who have many friends. And many wealthy people have few true friends who are not interested in their money.

Despite the difficulties of poverty in our world, we should never become so hardened that we simply turn away from hurting people. The Christian is not to despise his neighbor, but he is to have mercy on those who are less fortunate. Jesus became poor so that we might become rich. Let's do the same in whatever way God calls us to love the poor.

> *Dear Lord, help me to never judge the worth of a*
> *person by the size of his or her bank account.*

TODAY'S EVENING READING: Proverbs 14:20–35

61

DAY 15

Wisdom Verse

"A soft answer turns away wrath, but a harsh
word stirs up anger." —Proverbs 15:1

AN AMAZING FACT: Habitually angry people are three times more likely to suffer a heart attack.

Have you ever heard someone say, "I just lost it!" when he got really angry? What he misplaced was his rational thinking! Anger has a way of shutting down the part of our brains that helps us behave wisely. Being vexed potentially hijacks our ability to make good choices. People who cannot control their anger often hurt themselves and other people. I know this from personal experience. I used to have a hard time, when I was young, controlling my temper. I'd often get into fights at school.

Some people get angry because they feel they have been treated unfairly. Others get mad when they are under a lot of pressure. There are people who become irritated when they can't control certain situations. And some people are furious at injustices they see happening toward others. Whatever the reason, anger has the potential to be explosive and cause damage. Even cardiologists know the deadly effects on heart attack patients who do not deal with their anger.

The first story of sibling rivalry in the Bible reveals the devastating effects of anger. Cain and Abel were brothers who, through their father Adam, learned to worship God with an offering. Though God's instructions were clear about bringing a lamb, Cain was a farmer and decided to bring some of his own produce. Less messy? God accepted Abel's offering, but did not receive Cain's. The older brother became jealous of his younger sibling and murdered him. It's not a healthy picture.

You might feel your anger problem is not a big deal, but Jesus actually warns us, "Whoever is angry with his brother without a cause shall be in danger of the judgment" (Matthew 5:22). Christ actually associates anger with murder. It's as if Jesus is telling us that the end result of all anger leads to death, which is true when we break any of God's commandments.

The Prince of Peace can give you victory over your anger. He helped me. Through Bible study, prayer, memorizing Scripture, and the power of the Spirit, I've learned to not respond harshly to others who might be angry. That only stirs up a hornet's nest. It's much better to give a gentle answer. Soft responses sometimes come through silence and other times through carefully chosen words.

Dear Lord, remove all anger and hatred from my heart.
Fill me with peace, meekness, and contentment. Guide my
words today that I may be gentle with those I meet.

TODAY'S MORNING READING: Proverbs 15:1–15

DAY 15

EVENING

Wisdom Verse

*"A wise son makes a father glad, but a foolish man
despises his mother." —Proverbs 15:20*

AN AMAZING FACT: The total amount spent annually on Mother's
Day cards is $671 million. The total spent on flowers on Mother's Day
is $1.9 billion.

God made mothers with incredible love for their offspring. He
pre-wired them with a natural desire to protect their children,
even at the risk of their own lives. The Creator has programed
this sacrificial nature not just into human mothers, but also within the
maternal animal kingdom at large.

In the mountains of Northern California, we have a lot of black bears
that are generally harmless. On the few occasions when black bears have
attacked humans, it's usually because someone came between a mother
and her cubs. I even once heard of a car being ripped apart by a mother
bear because her cub was trapped inside when a well-meaning camper
tried to take it home. As the Bible says, "I will meet them like a bear
deprived of her cubs; I will tear open their rib cage" (Hosea 13:8).

All through the Bible, we see examples of a mother's love and
sacrifice. And this natural love, combined with the influence of a
godly mother, has changed history on many occasions. Mothers must
recognize the profound power they have in molding human souls, not
only for the difference they will make in this life, but also to prepare
them for eternity. As it is often said, "The hand that rocks the cradle
rules the world."

Paul reminds us, "Children, obey your parents in the Lord, for this is right. 'Honor your father and mother,' which is the first commandment with promise: 'that it may be well with you and you may live long on the earth' " (Ephesians 6:1–3).

Perhaps this is why our text for this evening calls a person who despises his mother a fool. Most mothers have given a tremendous amount of themselves to help their children be successful. Only a son who is blind to his mother's love will scorn her.

Someone once said, "It takes a village to raise a child." I categorically reject that. It might sound nice and reassuring to think the whole herd is watching out for everyone's children. But I believe that we have so much crime and decadence in our world because this "village" is really just a deceitful euphemism for the streets. It doesn't take a village to raise the child; it takes a mother and a father.

When a son or daughter pauses to recognize the sacrificial love of their parents, it brings gladness to the heart. Such respect fulfills the fifth commandment and honors our mothers and our fathers.

Thank you, Lord, for my parents and the good
qualities they have brought into my life. Teach me to
honor them and bring gladness to their hearts.

TODAY'S EVENING READING: Proverbs 15:16–33

DAY 16

Wisdom Verses

"As messengers of death is the king's wrath, but a wise man will appease it. In the light of the king's face is life, and his favor is like a cloud of the latter rain." —Proverbs 16:14, 15

AN AMAZING FACT: One of the most feared rulers in Roman history was Nero, who was known to capture and burn Christians in his garden to provide a source of light.

Nero's rule was known as one of tyranny and extravagance. Few historians have anything positive to say about his reign. He was Roman Emperor from AD 54 to 68. Nero was so fearful of losing power that he had his own mother and wife murdered and probably poisoned his stepbrother. Many believe he was responsible for the Great Fire of Rome and wanted space for his expanding palace. Christians were blamed for the conflagration, and thousands were martyred as a result.

The handsome young emperor started out better than he ended. His moderate rule changed in AD 62 when he became brutal and very immoral. He threw out his advisors and felt the need to be in complete control. Even the coins bearing his image began to show a somber man with fat cheeks and a protruding chin. Some Christians thought he was the antichrist and even associated his name with the number 666. What's clear is that Nero was one of the cruelest rulers of all time.

Certainly Solomon's advice in this morning's text would fit someone standing before Nero. When a ruler holds the power to take your life, you should walk carefully and speak with keen discernment before him. How much more this is true when the king is barbaric and rash. You would go to great lengths to avoid making him mad. Most of us will not cross paths with a king in our lifetimes, but we can apply this sage advice to other rulers in our lives—employers, police officers, managers, teachers, parents, and other supervisors.

Yet there is a King we should not overlook. Christ is our supreme ruler and a judgment day is coming. You might quickly say, "But Jesus isn't like Nero! He is kind and compassionate." Absolutely, but does this mean we should not seek to bring a smile to the face of God? Will there not come a time when the wrath of God will be shown to all sin and sinners?

The wrath of God (unlike man's wrath) was met when Jesus died for our sins. When we humbly accept His sacrifice and acknowledge our sins, it brings favor to the heart of our King.

Father in heaven, you are loving and patient, but
someday you will put an end to sin. I acknowledge my
sinfulness and accept your gift of salvation today.

TODAY'S MORNING READING: Proverbs 16:1–16

DAY 16

Wisdom Verse

*"The highway of the upright is to depart from evil; he who
keeps his way preserves his soul." —Proverbs 16:17*

AN AMAZING FACT: It is *not* true that one mile of every five miles of
the U.S. Interstate highway system must be straight enough to allow
planes to land on it. This is an urban legend.

Interstate highways in the United States are one of the blessings
of living in this country. I've traveled (and hitchhiked) on many
of these ribbons of concrete. Carefully chosen standards regulate
how these roads are constructed. For instance, all overpasses must have
a 16.5-foot vertical clearance. This was originally set in place to allow
some large military equipment to pass through. If this clearance cannot
be reached, then an exit and entry ramp needs to be in place to bypass
the overpass.

Our uninterrupted system of national highways didn't exist at
the turn of the 20th century. The first national road was created in
1811 and ran between Maryland and Illinois in order to help transport
immigrants. It wasn't until the late 1930s that President Franklin
Roosevelt pushed for a highway system as a way to provide jobs for
people. President Eisenhower made this a reality, and in 1954 money
was set aside to begin construction on the new roads.

Part of what drove Eisenhower to complete such a system of
highways occurred in 1919 when he was a young lieutenant colonel in
the army and part of the first transcontinental military convoy that

traveled from Washington, D.C., to San Francisco. It took them two months to complete the journey. His further experience during World War II showed him the advantages of the German autobahn network, which increased mobility and safety in that country.

Solomon also must have had an interest in well-maintained roadways. The Bible says, "Solomon gathered chariots and horsemen; he had one thousand four hundred chariots and twelve thousand horsemen, who he stationed in the chariot cities and with the king at Jerusalem" (1 Kings 10:26). In this golden era of Israel's history, the famous king raised the level of movement for his troops and workers to anywhere in his kingdom.

Real wisdom involves not only choosing the right road, but also knowing how to avoid the wrong ones. When we follow God's ways, it's as if we are raised up on a smooth, clean road, free of Satan's sidetracks. We may speed quickly past evil temptations and reach our destination without delay. We avoid exits that lead to sin and may move forward unhindered. Like riding on an interstate highway, we will be safe from the diversions of the enemy.

Lord, I choose to follow your ways. Though the devil will still try to pull me off the road to heaven, I choose to keep my eyes on you.

TODAY'S EVENING READING: Proverbs 16:17–33

DAY 17

Wisdom Verse

*"The beginning of strife is like releasing water; therefore stop
contention before a quarrel starts." —Proverbs 17:14*

AN AMAZING FACT: One of the worst dam failures in U.S. history
was the Johnstown flood of 1889 in Pennsylvania, which killed
2,209 people.

The dam, which was owned by the South Fork Fishing and
Hunting Club, was located 14 miles upstream from Johnstown.
This exclusive club counted Andrew Carnegie and Henry Clay
Frick among its members. It was a pleasure resort on Lake Conemaugh.
The reservoir created by the dam was completed in 1852, and little
maintenance was ever performed on it. In fact, when it broke through
once in 1862, someone removed drainage pipes and sold them for scrap.

By 1889, the dam was in desperate need of repairs. Then it began to
rain. It was late May and several days of extremely heavy rainfall, the
worst in recorded history for this area, began to fill the soggy dam to
overflowing. Twenty billion tons of water were pressing to be released.
Engineers were unsure how to manage the dam. Twice someone was
dispatched to telegraph the towns downstream, but previous false
alarms caused authorities to ignore the messages.

Finally, at 3:10 PM, the South Fork Dam collapsed. It only took 40
minutes for the entire lake to drain. The first town hit was South Fork.
It was situated on higher ground and four people were killed.

But as the wall of water rushed forward, it picked up debris, houses,
animals, trees, and factory materials. By the time it hit Johnstown, there

was so much rubbish that it looked more like a boiling mass of earth than water. The disaster was the largest loss of civilian life in America at the time—and it all started with a trickle.

It doesn't take much of an imagination to picture the parallel in our Bible passage between strife and a flood of water. Solomon warns that a little quarrel might seem innocent, like a small amount of water spilling over a dam. But what is happening underneath could work up a devastating burst. Have you ever noticed how a trivial squabble can grow into a major conflict? At the time it seemed it would just blow over. But in retrospect, a bit of resolution would have saved the relationship.

Take time to repair friendships. Give attention to discord and maintain harmony as much as possible. If you do, it will stop a torrent of anger that will destroy everything in its pathway.

> *Dear Jesus, thank you for stepping into the conflict*
> *of our world and bringing peace. Your mediation*
> *will someday put an end to all contention.*

TODAY'S MORNING READING: Proverbs 17:1–14

DAY 17

Wisdom Verse

"A merry heart does good, like medicine, but a broken spirit dries the bones." —Proverbs 17:22

AN AMAZING FACT: The only bone in the human body not connected to another is the hyoid, a U-shaped bone located at the base of the tongue.

I am always awed when I study the human body and how God constructed us. Even the skeletal system teaches us about the Creator, who lovingly put us together with this internal frame so that we wouldn't be just a blob on the floor!

We have 206 bones in our body; the thighbone is the largest and strongest, while the stapes (in the middle ear) is the smallest and lightest. Interestingly, this tiny bone is the only one that is fully grown at birth.

Bones not only hold our bodies upright and in place, but they allow different parts to move around. They also protect organs from being easily hurt. God created bones to be strong; in fact, a human bone is as strong as granite in supporting weight! One scientist determined that a block of bone the size of a matchbox can support nine tons.

Your skeletal system isn't just there to keep you sitting up straight in church. Inside your bones is a factory working to create blood cells. Even though this internal structure is strong, bones are very light. They are made up of calcium, phosphorus, sodium, and other minerals.

When you think about bones, you might first picture a dry skeleton hanging on a stand in biology class. Actually, bones are not a bunch of dry sticks—they're about 75 percent water. That means when Solomon says, "A broken spirit dries the bones," we should sit up and pay attention. Dry bones are indicators of really poor health.

Most people think the greatest impact on their health starts in their mouth with what they eat. That's certainly important, but we shouldn't overlook the connection between how we think and our health. The state of your mind impacts your health far more than you might realize. Many diseases begin not with the food on your plate, but with the grief or anxiety in your heart. It's not just what you're eating; it's what's eating you.

So put a genuine smile on your face. Ask God to give you a peaceful heart that is content and looks for the cheerful flowers on life's pathway. When you do this, your bones will thank you.

> *Lord, I choose to be joyful. I make the decision*
> *to set aside gloom and will practice having love,*
> *courage, and sympathy in my heart.*

TODAY'S EVENING READING: Proverbs 17:15–28

DAY 18

Wisdom Verse

"The name of the LORD is a strong tower; the righteous
run to it and are safe." —Proverbs 18:10

AN AMAZING FACT: The Windsor Castle is the longest-occupied palace in all of Europe.

Windsor Castle is also the largest inhabited castle in England. It's one of the residences of Queen Elizabeth II. She spends many weekends of the year there, using it for entertaining private and state groups. Located in the English county of Berkshire, it has a long history with the British royal family.

The castle was originally built in the 11th century after the Norman invasion of William the Conqueror. It was designed after the motte-and-bailey structure, with a raised mound surrounded by a ditch. A strong wall of timber and rock was created around a keep, often with a drawbridge, which led to a courtyard inside.

Towers were erected along the wall for defense purposes. In smaller castles, there might only be one tower that could house a few soldiers. Windsor began with a very simple plan, but over the last 950 years, new monarchs remodeled and created new additions. It now has three wards with the massive Round Tower occupying a central position. Many new towers were added over the years, including the Curfew, Edward III, Salisbury, Henry III, and the Garter Tower.

Windsor has survived many sieges since it was first built. In 1649 the English parliament almost voted to demolish the castle. A bill to destroy it lost by only one vote. It has been neglected and declared uninhabitable, but it now has been transformed into a luxurious palace. It has survived two World Wars. In fact, the royal family used the palace as a place of refuge during the bombings of World War II. In 1992 a large fire nearly destroyed a major portion of the castle.

In biblical times towers were built as places of refuge and safety, not just to make a fortress look nice. These strongholds could be more easily protected from approaching enemies since it placed defenders above attackers in a fortified structure. If a city wall was breached, people could run into a tower for safety. That's apparently the picture presented to us in this proverb. God's name is an impenetrable tower!

When Moses requested to see God, it was the Lord's name that was presented to him. God's name presents His character—gracious, loving, and compassionate (Exodus 34:6, 7). In other words, when we yield ourselves into God's hands, the Lord, who is merciful, will be our refuge and strength (Psalm 46:1).

> *Dear Lord, you are my fortress and hiding place. Today, as*
> *I face the enemy, I know that I am safe in your hands.*

TODAY'S MORNING READING: Proverbs 18:1–12

DAY 18

Wisdom Verses

*"Before destruction the heart of a man is haughty, and before
honor is humility. He who answers a matter before he hears
it, it is folly and shame to him." —Proverbs 18:12, 13*

AN AMAZING FACT: The largest invasion in the history of warfare was
Operation Barbarossa, the German's code name for invading the Soviet
Union during World War II. Three Axis army groups comprised four
million soldiers.

The size and scale of Nazi Germany's surprise invasion on Russia
beginning June 22, 1941, has no comparison. The huge number
of troops, combined with 3,580 tanks, 7,184 artillery guns, 1,830
planes, and 750,000 horses, simply boggles the mind. The German's
unbelievable plan was to cross a frontier of thousands of miles from
the Baltic to the Black Sea. Barbarossa was the greatest example of a
blitzkrieg ever attempted.

The strategy appeared to work at first. Adolf Hitler's ambitious but
cruel plan to conquer the USSR was not without cost. Almost 95 percent
of all German army casualties happened during this attack. Tactically,
the Germans appeared to win victory after victory, but their successes
stalled literally outside the gates of Moscow. The Soviets pushed back,
and the Wehrmacht never regained their grip. A bitter winter and
muddy roads didn't help.

The failure of Barbarossa was a turning point for the Third
Reich. Hitler's blunder of opening up the Eastern Front and pouring
a significant amount of forces into this operation created some of the

largest and deadliest battles in World War II. Conditions were horrific on both sides. The proud leader of Nazi Germany was eventually humbled.

The Bible text we look at this evening reminds me that those who lift themselves up too high will eventually fall. A haughty man exalts himself above everyone else. You can find many examples in the Bible of people who were arrogant, vain, and conceited. Saul refused the counsel of his advisors. King Zedekiah so resented the words of Jeremiah that he burned the scrolls sent to him. Even Judas, a disciple of Jesus, turned away from the gentle call of his Master; he believed he knew a better way.

Adolf Hitler was warned by his generals to not send troops east, to not enter into war with Russia, and to not drain the dwindling resources of the country. All of us, whether we are leaders or not, need to learn humility before receiving honor. We would do well to listen before we speak, to consider other viewpoints before insisting on our own plans. In the end, we will avoid destruction and save ourselves from shame.

> *"Humble yourselves in the sight of the Lord,*
> *and He will lift you up." —James 4:10*

TODAY'S EVENING READING: Proverbs 18:13–24

DAY 19

Wisdom Verse

"A false witness will not go unpunished, and he who
speaks lies will not escape." —Proverbs 19:5

AN AMAZING FACT: Han van Meegeren was one of the greatest art forgers of all time. He was so good that after being convicted of treason for selling what seemed liked authentic paintings to the Germans during World War II, he was required to paint a forgery to prove his innocence.

From childhood, van Meegeren wanted to be a famous artist. But critics denounced his work and, according to the budding artist, destroyed his career. So he came up with a plan to show others his skills. He forged paintings of some of the world's greatest artists. It worked. Soon his replications were regarded as some of the most superb in the world. His greatest copies were of the famous Dutch artist Johannes Vermeer. Slowly, his desire for praise led him into greed. His tireless attention to detail, faking cracks and aging paints, drove him to keep his work a secret.

But van Meegeren made a major mistake. During World War II, wealthy Dutchmen who wanted to prevent the Nazis from purchasing Dutch artwork began snatching up the artist's forgeries. Unfortunately, one fake painting ended up in the hands of a German officer and, after the war, it was discovered and traced back to van Meegeren. Since the piece was considered authentic, the artist was sentenced to death for being a conspirator and selling a "national treasure."

In order to save his life, van Meegeren confessed that he had painted a forgery. The courts did not believe him, and he eventually forged another painting in front of authorities to prove his "innocence." After this he was given a one-year sentence in prison. Han van Meegeren never served his term. Before being incarcerated, he died of a heart attack.

False witnesses painted a forged picture of Christ when Jesus stood before the Jewish leaders at an unlawful trial. The Sanhedrin court was so thirsty for blood that they hired bogus "witnesses" to testify against Christ. None of their contrived stories agreed. Finally, a statement made by Jesus was snatched and twisted into evidence of blasphemy against God. With this twisted shred, the Lord was led to Pilate and then the cross.

If you want to see an authentic portrait of God, study carefully the pages of Scripture, especially the gospels—where Jesus says, "He who has seen Me has seen the Father" (John 14:9). The life of Christ is more than a copy of His Father. He never once spoke a lie about God for He and the Father were One.

> *Today, dear Lord, may the image of Jesus be perfectly*
> *reflected in my life. Not a forgery, but authentic,*
> *with the Holy Spirit shining through my heart.*

TODAY'S MORNING READING: Proverbs 19:1–14

DAY 19

Wisdom Verse

"Listen to counsel and receive instruction, that you may
be wise in your latter days." —Proverbs 19:20

AN AMAZING FACT: Contrary to popular opinion, you can teach an old dog new tricks.

Actually, it is much easier to teach an old dog than it is to change habits in a human being. But the old adage about old dogs still has a nice ring to it, doesn't it? Most dog trainers will tell you the challenge of training your pet has less to do with the animal at the end of the collar and more to do with the one holding the leash. (I think the saying was created by someone as an excuse for not trying something new and fresh!)

How many times have you heard someone say, "I'm too old to change!" People probably thought that about Harlan David Sanders. When he was young, Harlan worked many different jobs. He did farming, worked on a steamboat, and was even an insurance salesman. At 40 he opened a service station and sold chicken dinners to his patrons. As the years went by, his way of preparing chicken became more and more popular, so he finally opened a restaurant. When a new freeway pulled future customers away from his business, he opened a franchise and Kentucky Fried Chicken was born. The Colonel was 65 years old.

I could expound on Ray Kroc, who started McDonald's at 52; Laura Ingalls Wilder, who published her first *Little House* book at age 65; or Grandma Moses, who began painting at age 75. Benjamin Franklin signed the U.S. Constitution at age 81. Golda Meir became Israel's prime minister when she was 70. Ronald Reagan became President of the United States just 16 days before his 70th birthday. And Peter Mark Roget published his well-used thesaurus at the age of 73.

Still, I think Moses rises to the top of all leaders in Scripture for his service to God in his latter years. His call at the burning bush happened when he was 80 years old. In his first 40 years, he learned the ways of the Egyptians. In his second 40 years, he had to unlearn many things. Then, from the ages of 80 to 120, this intelligent and humble man led Israel to the border of the Promised Land.

Solomon wrote the book of Proverbs early in his reign. The wisdom he first lived by led Israel into a golden era. The king pointed people to God as the source of all wisdom. Had this wise man taken his own medicine, he would have left a strong legacy to the last days of his life.

Dear Lord, I commit all of my years to you and
pray that my search for wisdom and counsel will
continue until my final days or until you come.

TODAY'S EVENING READING: Proverbs 19:15–29

DAY 20

Wisdom Verse

"Even a child is known by his deeds, whether what
he does is pure and right." —Proverbs 20:11

AN AMAZING FACT: The first and largest building in the world to use a significant amount of glass was the Crystal Palace, constructed in London for the Great Exhibition in 1851.

In those days, cast plate glass was a new invention, and when designs were being gathered for an exhibition hall to be built in Hyde Park, Sir Joseph Paxton, a famous English garden designer, struck on the idea of a large building of cast-iron and glass that would not need artificial lighting. Visitors were astonished with the clear walls and ceilings, which was the most found in any building at the time.

The first glass windows were anything but clear. Blown glass bubbles were originally flattened into panes in the last part of the third century. By the 1550s, glass windows were becoming more common but were still considered a luxury of the super-wealthy. Leaded windows were introduced in the 17th century, and by the 19th century engineers were beginning to create large, flat, clear, and strong glass panes, first used in conservatories and greenhouses.

Our text for this morning brings out the simple clarity of a child's life. Children have little to hide and, like peering into a glass house, we simply observe their behaviors to understand their characters. Adults are much more sophisticated about hiding their thoughts and motives. Yet if we study a person's behavior carefully, we can see into their soul and know their character.

Jesus taught, "Let your 'Yes' be 'Yes,' and your 'No,' 'No.' For whatever is more than these is from the evil one" (Matthew 5:37). Christ's words suggest that long, elaborate statements and swearing oaths are unnecessary for the Christian, whose pledges should be simple, plain, and trustworthy.

Nathanael was someone in the Bible who exhibited a transparent character. His life was not clouded and obscure. Jesus said of him, "Behold, an Israelite indeed, in whom is no deceit!" (John 1:47). This disciple was genuine and served God with a sincere heart. He lived in harmony with God's will and was not a hypocrite. This representative of Jesus left us an example of living an open and honest life into which others could freely look. He had nothing to hide.

Like a simple, open child who is straightforward in his actions, so should we live transparent lives for God. Like a crystal temple, others will look at us and see within our hearts the image of Jesus.

Lord, today I invite you to wash the windows of
my heart and send your Spirit to live within me
so that others might more clearly see you.

TODAY'S MORNING READING: Proverbs 20:1–15

DAY 20

Wisdom Verse

*"Blows that hurt cleanse away evil, as do stripes the
inner depths of the heart." —Proverbs 20:30*

AN AMAZING FACT: Women have more pain receptors in their skin
than men.

Scientists have also discovered that women have more nerve
receptors overall than men. For example, a woman has 34 nerve
fibers per square centimeter on their face, whereas men have an
average of 17. Of course, then there is the big debate on whether men or
women can tolerate pain more. If you have ever seen a woman give birth
to a baby, you might think women can tolerate just about anything!

Not all pain is alike. Some pain is physical, some emotional, and
some is called "phantom" pain, which comes from a "phantom" body
part that is no longer there because of amputation. Severe pain can be
caused by migraine headaches and kidney stones. More mild pain might
come from biting your tongue or getting a paper cut. Yet all pain serves a
purpose: to let us know something bad is happening.

So how is it that Solomon can tell us that "blows that hurt cleanse
away evil?" Because sometimes a remedy for a problem is temporarily
painful but necessary in order to bring healing—such as discipline to
warn a child playing in the street to prevent a tragic car accident. Or as
a boil that needs to be lanced and cleansed, there are sins in our life that
require treatment and cleansing.

When my children were small, sometimes they would get a sliver
of wood under their skin. There was always the struggle of whether to

leave it alone to fester or let Daddy pull it out—which could be briefly painful. Of course, in the long run, the momentary pain brought more lasting relief.

Nathan the prophet once brought some deep pain to King David. The spiritual blow took place after his great sin with Bathsheba. The man of God stood without flinching before the monarch and with piercing words struck the heart of David, pointing out his transgression by saying, "You are the man!" (2 Samuel 12:7). The lash saved the king, who repented and turned to God, begging for a clean heart.

If we would be saved in God's kingdom, we would welcome God's discipline to cleanse our minds and hearts. We would pray, "Search me, O God, and know my heart; try me, and know my anxieties; and see if there is any wicked way in me, and lead me in the way everlasting" (Psalm 139:23, 24). Then we would allow the Spirit to work deep in our lives, even if it is painful.

It always lessens the blow when we draw near to the one who holds the rod.

Dear Jesus, I pray that I will be aware of sin creeping into my life and turn to the Bible, allowing truth to cut anything from my life that keeps me from being more like you.

TODAY'S EVENING READING: Proverbs 20:16–30

DAY 21

Wisdom Verse

"The king's heart is in the hand of the Lord, like the rivers of water; He turns it wherever He wishes." —Proverbs 21:1

AN AMAZING FACT: The length of the Mississippi River is debated because measurements can change from year to year due to floods that change the course of the river.

The team at Itasca State Park in Minnesota says the Mississippi River is 2,552 miles long. The U.S. Geologic Survey published the length as 2,300 miles, and the Mississippi National River and Recreation Area suggests the length is 2,350 miles. Each of these groups uses a different method to determine the river's length, which can also change year to year from flooding conditions.

One historic course change for the Mississippi took place suddenly in March 1876, when it took a new turn near the town of Reverie, Tennessee. When the border between Arkansas and Tennessee was put in place in 1795, the boundary followed the middle of the Mississippi River. At this time the river ran northwest of the town. But after the change it ran southeast of Reverie, cutting it off from Tipton County. Today water sometimes runs on both sides of the town, and technically the land for Reverie is called "Island No. 35."

Big rivers are not easy things to turn, but that's how Cyrus the Great, king of Persia, captured ancient Babylon. Belshazzar, the Babylonian king, was holding a feast to the gods of his country, using the sacred vessels they had captured from the Jewish temple. As they celebrated, suddenly a mysterious hand appeared and wrote on the wall. Daniel the prophet was called to interpret the writing and declared that the end of Belshazzar's kingdom had arrived. (See Daniel 5.)

It came as a total surprise. The walls of Babylon were thought to be impenetrable. The Euphrates River flowed under the walls and through the city, and where it passed under the wall there were metal gates to prevent intruders from entering. Cyrus commanded his soldiers upstream to divert the river into a dry lakebed; eventually, the level dropped low enough for soldiers to enter under the river gates and conquer the city.

A king holds great power in his hands. His position and decisions can impact many people. But even the most boastful monarchs in Scripture, such as the pharaoh during the time of Moses or Belshazzar in Daniel's time, are still subject to God's Spirit and providence. In what seems like an almost unbelievable turn of events, Cyrus, the king who conquered Babylon, later gave an order to restore the temple in Jerusalem. God changed the course of a king's heart, and He can do the same today in your heart if you are willing.

Lord, you are the rightful King of the entire universe. Please direct my life today.

TODAY'S MORNING READING: Proverbs 21:1–15

DAY 21

Wisdom Verse

"The horse is prepared for the day of battle, but
deliverance is from the Lord." —Proverbs 21:31

AN AMAZING FACT: Ten million soldiers died in World War I, along
with eight million military horses.

Historians believe that horses have been used in warfare since
as far back as 5,000 years ago. Along the way, their utility has
increased with the creation of the saddle, stirrup, horse collar,
harness, and chariot. Some were ridden in cavalry charges, while others
merely pulled wagons or artillery.

World War I was a transition in the use of the horse. Because of
the advancement of machine guns, they were used less and less on the
battlefield, but they began to be used more for carrying messengers and
pulling supply wagons and ambulances. They could often get through
deep mud and over rough terrain better than motorized vehicles.

War is especially brutal on horses. They are struck by gunfire and
are often left on the battlefield to die. During the American Civil War,
injured horses were often used by soldiers to shield themselves from
bullets as they advanced forward. Horses during World War I were
worked till they dropped, and many were poisoned by gas. Horses are
often the unsung heroes in war.

Today we mostly see warhorses in reenactments of battle scenes or
in parades. But even in biblical times, it was a great advantage to have
horses as part of your armament. The Egyptians pursued the Israelites

using horses and chariots at the time of the exodus. Solomon was known to have 4,000 horse stalls and 12,000 horsemen (2 Chronicles 9:25).

Even though having horses was thought to greatly increase your odds in warfare, Solomon tells us that without God on our side, it doesn't matter how much military might we have. The Bible is filled with examples where God's people went into the battle trusting the Lord and were victorious over larger forces that included horses and chariots.

That's why the weakest saint kneeling in a gutter is mightier than the proudest person riding on the tallest horse. The tipping point is whether you have the Lord's power in your arsenal.

Solomon's father wrote, "Some trust in chariots, and some in horses; but we will remember the name of the LORD our God" (Psalm 20:7). And also, "A horse is a vain hope for safety; neither shall it deliver any by its great strength" (Psalm 33:17). Though we have a responsibility to prepare for battling the enemy, the ultimate deliverance comes only from the power of God.

Dear Jesus, I choose to be on your side. As I
do my part in exercising my faith, all victory
comes through my connection to you.

TODAY'S EVENING READING: Proverbs 21:16–31

Wisdom Verse

*"The rich rules over the poor, and the borrower is
servant to the lender." —Proverbs 22:7*

AN AMAZING FACT: Sears makes more money today off credit interest than selling merchandise. But back in 1910, its own catalog stated, "Buying on credit is folly."

L ikewise, the founder of J.C. Penney hated debt, yet today the store makes millions off their credit cards. Even Henry Ford didn't offer financing for the first 10 years of the Ford Motor Company, because he felt credit was a lazy man's way of making purchases.

Of course, the United States has a serious problem with credit and credit cards. Five billion credit card solicitations are mailed out each year nationwide, and about 0.4 percent of these offers are accepted. Eighty percent of American households have at least one credit card, and the average number of cards held by most people is seven!

To put the dollars in perspective, the average household credit card debt is about $9,300, and most people pay about 16 percent on all outstanding balances each month. The total credit card debt in the United States is about $665 billion on bank credit cards and about $105 billion on store and gas credit cards.

Today's proverb is obviously one that more of us need to hear. Whenever someone loans a person money, it puts the relationship into a ruler-servant status. It really doesn't matter if it is your local bank or your best friend. Loaning people money changes the dynamics of how you view each other. Most of the time when we make a loan to a family member or friend, we think we are being kind and helpful, but in the long run it often unravels and hurts the relationship. It's better to not lend and avoid the long-term stress.

The deeper issue is that many people are controlled by their materialism and instant gratification, not wisdom. We want things right now; we can't wait. But learning to earn and pay for something by the sweat of your brow teaches patience and gives you satisfaction in your efforts. You are not a slave to anyone and free to live and serve the Lord without strings attached to your income. You'll be able to make more and give more to His cause!

Don't live like 90 percent of the people in our country who purchase things they cannot afford and then forever pay absurd and never-ending interest. Follow the wisdom of Solomon. Avoid debt as if it were the plague and live with the peace God intended you to have in your life.

> *Dear Lord, you never intended any of your children to*
> *be slaves to the world. May I live and save and spend*
> *so that I may serve only one Master—Jesus Christ.*

TODAY'S MORNING READING: Proverbs 22:1–16

DAY 22

Wisdom Verse

"Do not remove the ancient landmark which
your fathers have set." —Proverbs 22:28

AN AMAZING FACT: The boundary stones marking the District of Columbia are the oldest federally placed monuments in the United States.

On July 16, 1790, the Residence Act authorized President George Washington to choose a 100-square-mile site for the nation's capital. Under his direction, Secretary of State Thomas Jefferson selected Major Andrew Ellicott to survey a 10-mile square on the Potomac River between Alexandria, Virginia, and Williamsport, Maryland. Ellicot began his work on February 12, 1791.

With the help of Benjamin Banneker, the first boundary stone was placed on the southernmost point of the D.C. diamond. Then working clockwise, the team placed 39 additional stones. Each block of Aquia Creek sandstone, which weighed about a half ton, was chiseled with inscriptions indicating the territory it faced, the year it was placed, and a compass reading.

Over the years, four of the forty original stones were lost. In a 2011 survey using modern technology, the locations of the stones were found to be remarkably accurate, sometimes off by only six feet! Some of the original markers are located in people's yards, one in a cemetery, another in a median strip, and still another in a church parking lot. Each year a group of "D.C. Diamond Hikers" walks the diamond to commemorate these ancient landmarks.

Today we can accurately check property boundary lines with GPS readings, but in Bible times all they had were ancient landmark stones that were established in place with sacred covenants. When the Israelites entered the Promised Land, instructions were given to respect boundaries: "You shall not remove your neighbor's landmark, which the men of old have set, in your inheritance which you will inherit in the land that the LORD your God is giving you to possess" (Deuteronomy 19:14). In fact, people were cursed if they moved them (27:17).

God was the first surveyor on our planet. "Where were you when I laid the foundations of the earth? ... Who determined its measurements? Surely you know! Or who stretched the line upon it?" (Job 38:4, 5). More precisely, God's Word and law provide the true unmovable landmarks of life.

I choose to stand by the solid precepts found in the Bible. The measurement and placement of these principles are exactly where the Lord wants them to be.

> *Dear Jesus, thank you for the Bible, the unmistakable*
> *source of truth. As I study your Word, I rest assured that*
> *the teachings of Scripture are perfect in their placement.*

TODAY'S EVENING READING: Proverbs 22:17–29

Wisdom Verses

"When you sit down to eat with a ruler, consider carefully
what is before you; and put a knife to your throat if you
are a man given to appetite. Do not desire his delicacies,
for they are deceptive food." —Proverbs 23:1–3

AN AMAZING FACT: "Old Tom Parr" was an Englishman who is said to have lived for 152 years (1483–1635). Naturally, some doubt the stories of his extensive age.

Thomas Parr was thought to have been born in 1483 during the reign of King Richard III and is said to have lived to the age of 152, having seen ten sovereigns on the throne during his long life, including the 50-year reign of Queen Elizabeth I.

Old Parr, as he was sometimes called, became a celebrity in England as news of his great age spread. Special portraits of him were painted, and he was eventually brought to London to meet King Charles I in 1635.

The king invited Parr to the palace and inquired as to what Thomas owed his long life, and the old farmer said that he had worked hard and lived on a simple diet of oatmeal; potatoes; coarse, hard bread; and small drink, generally sour whey.

But Old Parr was not accustomed to the rich food served at the palace, and that night, after dining on the king's delicacies, legend has it that he became very ill and died. William Harvey, the physician who performed a post-mortem on Parr's body, could find no apparent cause for death and assumed Thomas died of overexposure. King Charles felt so terrible having killed Britain's oldest citizen with his food that he commanded the deceased should be buried in Westminster Abbey.

Rich delicacies are not the typical fare of people who live to ripe old ages. Even the Bible points this out through the story of Daniel and his friends, who were shipped off to Babylon and chosen to be trained in the king's court as future leaders in their new country. "But Daniel purposed in his heart that he would not defile himself with the portion of the king's delicacies, nor with the wine which he drank; therefore he requested of the chief of the eunuchs that he might not defile himself" (Daniel 1:8).

God honored Daniel's choice to avoid eating the unclean Babylonian food. Chapter 1 of Daniel ends by telling us that Daniel and his friends were 10 times wiser than the other counselors of Babylon and that Daniel lived nearly 100 years. So also may our guarded appetites lead to wiser, longer, and more abundant life!

> *Father in heaven, guide all my choices in what I eat*
> *and drink. Help me guard my appetite and take only*
> *that which will help me grow strong in you.*

TODAY'S MORNING READING: Proverbs 23:1–16

DAY 23

Wisdom Verses

"Who has woe? Who has sorrow? Who has contentions?
Who has complaints? Who has wounds without cause?
Who has redness of eyes? Those who linger long at the wine,
those who go in search of mixed wine." —Proverbs 23:29, 30

AN AMAZING FACT: An alcohol-related problem affects one in every four U.S. homes.

The uncontrollable desire for alcohol consumes about 14 million Americans. About 47 percent of industrial injuries and 40 percent of industrial fatalities are linked to alcohol consumption. Drinking also can increase violent behavior and accounts for 49 percent of murders, 52 percent of rapes, 21 percent of suicides, and 60 percent of child abuse cases. Of course, of all fatal accidents on the roads, over 50 percent involve alcohol.

Staggeringly, more than 50 percent of the people who are in prisons, hospitals, and mental institutions are there because of crime, illness, and birth defects related to alcohol. A wise Christian should have nothing to do with this drug.

There are basically four elements that indicate a person is struggling with alcohol. First, there is a strong craving to drink. Next, there is a loss of control to stop drinking once a person has begun. Then there is a physical dependence on alcohol, causing withdrawal symptoms that can be relieved by another drink. Finally, there is the issue of tolerance—the need to drink increasing amounts of alcohol to get a "high."

Proverbs accurately describes the harmful effects of drinking alcohol. It warns that alcohol "bites like a serpent, and stings like a viper" (Proverbs 23:31, 32). Like all the destructive temptations of Satan, drinking liquor is portrayed as cool and smart and something that the beautiful do. But it is foolish and ugly. It not only destroys our capacity to think and act wisely, it harms those around us.

It's not just the book of Proverbs that warns us regarding the evil consequences of alcohol: "Do not be drunk with wine, in which is dissipation; but be filled with the Spirit" (Ephesians 5:18). And, "Woe to those who rise early in the morning, that they may follow intoxicating drink; who continue until night, till wine inflames them!" (Isaiah 5:11).

Biblical wisdom teaches us to firmly avoid alcohol. If you or a loved one has been in the grips of drinking, admit the problem and get help. God wants you to be free from the serpent's bite.

Dear Lord, please guide me away from harmful substances that lead me away from you. I cannot conquer the enemy on my own, but I believe through Christ that all things are possible.

TODAY'S EVENING READING: Proverbs 23:17–35

DAY 24

Wisdom Verses

*"My son, eat honey because it is good, and the honeycomb
which is sweet to your taste; so shall the knowledge of wisdom
be to your soul; if you have found it, there is a prospect, and
your hope will not be cut off." —Proverbs 24:13, 14*

AN AMAZING FACT: Bees must visit about two million flowers and
travel 55,000 miles to make one pound of honey.

There is an art to finding wild beehives—tricks to locating the delicious, sweet substance we love to eat. The method basically focuses on following a "beeline." When bees have collected their fill of pollen, they head straight home. That means if you set up a dish of homemade nectar (a mix of water and sugar), you can actually watch a bee load up and then take off. Noticing the direction of the bee will give you an idea where his nest is located.

You can sharpen the results by timing the length between trips of this first bee. It will give you an idea of how far away the bee tree is located. You can also triangulate coordinates by setting up more than one dish or plate and then plot them on a map. Some people even use a GPS unit or computer programs to narrow down the location. Searching for wild honey might be a little easier later in the summer and early fall when flowers are fewer. Of course, you also need to beware that you might be led to your neighbor's beehives!

The Bible tells us that Jonathan once ate some wild honey he found in the woods. He said, "Look now, how my countenance has brightened because I tasted a little of this honey (1 Samuel 14:29). This was also the food of John the Baptist.

Finding wild honey takes patience and perseverance, but the rewards are sweet. So it is with the person searching for wisdom. The Scriptures teach that the law of the Lord is "sweeter also than honey and the honeycomb" (Psalm 19:10). When we are persistent in looking for Jesus, the source of all truth, we will have a future full of hope and sweet blessings.

When Jeremiah wrote to the captives in Babylon who were carried off by Nebuchadnezzar, the words from God spoke of searching and hope. "And you will seek Me and find Me, when you search for Me with all your heart" (Jeremiah 29:13). There are no tricks in finding the Lord. Humble yourself, pray to Him, and spend time every day in the Bible. Jesus will lead you in a beeline to heaven.

"Tis so sweet to trust in Jesus, just to take Him at His word; just to rest upon His promise, just to know, 'Thus says the Lord.'"

TODAY'S MORNING READING: Proverbs 24:1–16

DAY 24

Wisdom Verse

"He who gives a right answer kisses the lips." —Proverbs 24:26

AN AMAZING FACT: The average person spends about 336 hours of his or her life kissing.

Pressing your lips against another person or object has a variety of meanings in different cultures. Depending on the context, a kiss can show love and affection, be a greeting, or be a ritual demonstrating devotion. In the right context, kissing can be good for you. Babies seem to grow and thrive when given appropriate physical affection. Husbands who kiss their wives goodbye each day before going to work live longer and the wives experience fewer health problems.

You can find many references to kissing in the Bible. Isaac kissed his son Jacob (Genesis 27:26). After anointing David with oil, Samuel kissed him to show his fealty to the new king (1 Samuel 10:1). Mary Magdalene kissed the feet of Jesus to show gratitude and worship (Luke 7:38). And there are even a few references to the traditional romantic kiss. "Let him kiss me with the kisses of his mouth—for your love is better than wine" (Song of Solomon 1:2).

According to our text for this evening, how would a right answer be like a kiss on the lips? Some translations interpret a "right" answer as one that is honest or even frank. "Giving an honest answer is a sign of true friendship" (Proverbs 24:26 CEV). "An honest answer is as pleasing as a kiss on the lips" (ERV). This verse stands in contrast to one that precedes it: "He who says to the wicked, 'You are righteous,' him the people will curse; nations will abhor him" (v. 24).

When a person speaks the truth, especially in times when it might be painful, it is a blessing. Dishonest kings and two-faced leaders cannot be trusted. Like a sincere kiss, which shows affection and love, an honest answer shows how another is concerned for our welfare. "But those who rebuke the wicked will have delight, and a good blessing will come upon them" (v. 25).

Then, of course, there is one kiss in the Bible that led to the death of two people. Judas betrayed Jesus with a false kiss of friendship (Luke 22:47, 48). Christ was then taken, tried, and crucified. Judas, who realized the injustice of this action, went out and hung himself. A gesture of deep friendship had been turned into a breach of trust. May our words and kisses always speak the truth! "Faithful are the wounds of a friend; but the kisses of an enemy are deceitful" (Proverbs 27:5, 6).

Dear Jesus, by your grace I will guard my words as much as my expressions of affection. May I speak the truth to those around me as an act of kindness.

TODAY'S EVENING READING: Proverbs 24:17–34

DAY 25

Wisdom Verse

"Whoever falsely boasts of giving is like clouds
and wind without rain." —Proverbs 25:14

AN AMAZING FACT: "Cloud seeding" is an experimental method used to cause rain to fall; silver iodide or dry ice has been dumped into clouds in an effort to change its properties and create a rain shower.

If you are a farmer experiencing a severe drought, you might try just about anything to get rain. Efforts to change the weather and increase precipitation have led some scientists, meteorologists, and even commercial companies to develop a way to encourage water to fall from the sky. The original idea was to "seed" clouds with tiny particles whose electrical charge would bring together the cloud's water droplets. When enough droplets come together, their weight would cause rain to drop.

Most commercial outfits emphasize they cannot break droughts but only enhance the conditions in the atmosphere and make it more likely to rain. When thunderstorms approach, these rain makers send up planes to seed the "inflow" part of the clouds that suck up moisture, hoping the particles collide with water vapor and condense into raindrops. Recent research has shown that airplanes that simply pass through clouds appear to create more rain and snow as they punch holes in the clouds, creating a super-cooling effect on water molecules.

Though there are many skeptics on the process of rainmaking, the desire for water to come down from the sky has existed for thousands of years. The most famous biblical weather change during a drought took place during the time of King Ahab. When Elijah confronted the wicked king, he said, "As the LORD God of Israel lives, before whom I stand, there shall not be dew nor rain these years, except at my word" (1 Kings 17:1). No matter how many rain dances and spells were performed by the prophets of Baal, it did not rain.

But something changed. When Elijah had a showdown with these false prophets (whose gods supposedly controlled the weather) on top of Mount Carmel, God exposed the emptiness of their religion. After they were destroyed, Elijah promised Ahab it would rain again. Then he prayed for rain. Seven times he asked his servant to look toward the sea until a rain cloud appeared. Rain eventually drenched the land.

Like Ahab's false prophets, people who boast and make promises of generosity but do not follow through are like clouds that pass over a drought stricken land yet never rain. They bring only dashed hopes and withered expectations. As followers of the Lord, let's always follow through on our pledges to give.

Father in heaven, just as I can count on your
Word, may I live a trustworthy life.

TODAY'S MORNING READING: Proverbs 25:1–14

DAY 25

Wisdom Verses

"If your enemy is hungry, give him bread to eat; and if he is thirsty, give him water to drink; for so you will heap coals of fire on his head, and the LORD will reward you." —Proverbs 25:21, 22

AN AMAZING FACT: In ancient Egypt, a person guilty of some wrongdoing might carry a pan of burning coals on his head as a sign of repentance.

I once read a story about a boy at summer camp who received a box of cookies from home. He ate a few and then put the rest under his bed. The next day they were gone. His counselor saw another boy eating them down by the lake, so he approached the first boy and said, "I know who stole your cookies. Would you like to teach him a lesson?" The boy agreed, so the counselor said, "Ask your mom to send you another box of cookies."

When the new box arrived, the counselor encouraged the boy to go share them with the boy who had stolen his cookies. He hesitated, "But why? Shouldn't he be punished?" But the counselor insisted he find the boy and try to share with him anyway. Later the counselor saw the two boys walking with their arms around each other's shoulders. The kindness of the first boy so touched the one who stole the cookies that he insisted his new friend take his pocketknife as payment for his crime.

I think the hunger in the heart of the little boy who stole the cookies might have been more than physical. Perhaps he didn't hear from home very much. So by looking beyond the obvious wrong, the first boy touched the heart of this robber and made him a friend. Even though the boy had the right to demand retribution, the counselor's approach created a companion. Paul said, "Do not be overcome by evil, but overcome evil with good" (Romans 12:21).

David once had the right to execute justice toward an evil man named Nabal. After David and his men protected Nabal's flocks and herds for months, they requested some supplies, but David's men were spurned by Nabal, who even threatened them. The future king of Israel was enraged and marched his troops to teach this selfish man a thing or two. But Nabal's wife got wind of her husband's selfish response and prepared a large supply of food for David and his men. Then she intercepted David and humbly pleaded for mercy. It touched David's heart, and he received her gifts and turned back from his mission of vengeance.

When we show kindness to our enemies, it has the potential to bring remorse, to "burn" their conscience. God rewards us when we seek to show love, even to our foes.

> *Thank you, Jesus, for showing kindness toward me though I*
> *have often spurned your love. Help me to love my enemies.*

TODAY'S EVENING READING: Proverbs 25:15–28

DAY 26

Wisdom Verse

*"As snow in the summer and rain in harvest, so honor
is not fitting for a fool." —Proverbs 26:1*

AN AMAZING FACT: The fastest temperature rise ever recorded was
in Spearfish, South Dakota, on January 22, 1943, when it climbed 49
degrees in only two minutes.

There have been many more strange and amazing weather
records set since the use of accurate instruments and official
confirmations. For instance, the most consecutive number of
days above 100 degrees happened in Marble Bar, Western Australia,
from October 31, 1923, to April 7, 1924. That totals 160 days! (I wonder
if they also broke records for selling the most lemonade.) The world
record for the highest temperature ever recorded was at the Furnace
Creek Ranch in Death Valley, California, where the thermometer hit an
astounding 134 degrees on July 10, 1913.

At the other end of the spectrum, the coldest temperature ever
recorded on our planet was at the Vostok Station in the Antarctica on
July 21, 1983, where it was minus 128.6 degrees. The fastest temperature
drop was 49 degrees in 15 minutes in Rapid City, South Dakota, on
January 10, 1911.

When it comes to precipitation, the most rain to ever fall in one
minute was 1.5 inches in Barot, Guadeloupe, on November 26, 1970.
The most rain in less than one hour was 12 inches in 42 minutes in Holt,
Missouri, on June 22, 1947. And the most rain in one year was 1,042
inches in Cherrapunji, India, in 1860. That's almost 87 feet!

What grabs our attention about unusual weather? Day after day, the weather generally tends to be pretty predictable. Farmers count on this when timing their planting and harvest. So if it snows in the summer or rains during harvest time, this out of place weather can destroy crops. That's just what Solomon is saying when describing the idea of honoring fools.

I am sorry to say that in today's culture, we regularly honor people who lack moral judgment. Celebrities who make millions of dollars and have affairs make the front page of the news. Business leaders who steal, sports heroes who use drugs, comedians who pour filth from their mouths, and politicians who break the law are sometimes excused and adored because of their other accomplishments. We're a little mixed up when we applaud fools. It makes about as much sense as a snowstorm at Furnace Creek in July.

> *Lord, may I only honor those who live wisely and respect*
> *those who demonstrate good values by how they behave.*

TODAY'S MORNING READING: Proverbs 26:1–12

DAY 26

Wisdom Verse

*"Whoever digs a pit will fall into it, and he who rolls a
stone will have it roll back on him." —Proverbs 26:27*

AN AMAZING FACT: The worst mining accident in U.S. history was
the Monongah coal mine explosion, which claimed 362 lives.

D igging tunnels underground is risky business. Hundreds of
miners around the world die each year from mining accidents,
especially among coal miners. Sometimes poisonous gases
enter the mine, or explosive natural gases are ignited. Dust explosions
have been common, along with flooding, collapsing, and equipment
that failed to work properly. The worst mining accident in world history
was the Benxihu Colliery in China in 1942. It claimed the lives of
1,549 workers.

Around the turn of the 20th century, mining accidents were quite
common. In 1907, when the Monongah explosion took place, there were
18 other coal mine disasters. Public outrage finally prompted congress
to create the Bureau of Mines. Since then, year by year, the number
of disasters has dropped dramatically through ongoing research and
education in mine safety. A collapse is still the biggest worry, accounting
for 50 percent of fatal injuries.

Solomon warns us in our text for this evening, "Whoever digs a pit
will fall into it." This is talking about someone who digs a pit to trap an
innocent person; he will fall into his own pit. Or perhaps someone who
tries to roll a large stone down a hill to crush someone, she might find

the stone will rock back on her first. Like a boomerang or a collapsing mine, the one who does wrong toward others will have justice return on his own head—if not in this life, then certainly in the final judgment. The risk is much greater than digging for coal or moving large rocks.

Queen Esther saw the truth of this proverb come true when the wicked Haman tried to subtly destroy all of God's people and hang her cousin, Mordecai, on a large gallows he had built. When the sinister plot was uncovered, the queen fasted and prayed and then approached the king who brought swift justice to Haman. He was executed that day on the gallows he had built to hang Mordecai. Haman's evil plot ricocheted back on his own head.

When we break God's law, there is a consequence to our actions. Unless we repent and confess our transgressions and accept the sheltering grace of God, we will receive the just rewards of our iniquity— death. I am so thankful that Jesus went into the pit and bore the weight of sin so that we can be rescued.

> *O Lord, I have fallen into my own pit of sin.*
> *Please reach down your saving hand and lift me*
> *up and place my feet on solid ground.*

TODAY'S EVENING READING: Proverbs 26:13–28

DAY 27

Wisdom Verse

"A prudent man foresees evil and hides himself; the simple
pass on and are punished." —Proverbs 27:12

AN AMAZING FACT: The mimic octopus of Indonesia can change to any pattern or color and even match the shape and features of other animals or surroundings.

This octopus is the only species known that can impersonate so many different animals, and most of those it mimics—lionfish, jellyfish, sea snake, and many others—are poisonous, making it an excellent survival tactic.

Wouldn't it be nice if we could hide and camouflage ourselves from the allure of temptation as easily as the animals that can disguise themselves? As Christians, we encounter many situations from which we should run and take cover. The Bible tells us to "flee sexual immorality" (1 Corinthians 6:18), "flee from idolatry" (1 Corinthians 10:14), and—speaking of pride, greed, and others sins—"flee these things" (1 Timothy 6:11).

Part of fleeing from evil is avoiding temptation. Jesus told His disciples they needed to watch and pray in order to avoid temptation. This is not to say that temptation is sin. We know that Christ was tempted, and we also know that He was sinless. Obviously, some temptation is unavoidable. But knowing your weaknesses and avoiding situations where you could easily be lured into wrongdoing is simply using the wisdom that God gave you; it's common sense. For instance, if a man knows he is tempted by alcohol, he knows he will be putting himself on Satan's ground if he visits a bar.

Where temptation can't be avoided, Jesus will provide the power to resist it. Because Jesus suffered temptation on this earth, He understands our problems perfectly and is able to give us just the help we need when we are tempted. He is ready and able to strengthen us. If we trust in Him, He will never leave us to battle temptation on our own. He wants to empower us!

The prudent man in our verse above hides himself from evil. So where can we hide ourselves? Where can we take cover and be protected from the immorality that surrounds us? "For in the time of trouble He shall hide me in His pavilion; in the secret place of His tabernacle He shall hide me; He shall set me high upon a rock" (Psalm 27:5).

The Word of God clearly teaches that we should hide in Christ; God is our only "safety zone." And we don't need to wait until we think we're in trouble to run to Him. Make Him your constant refuge. If we remain in Him, we will be victorious!

Dear Lord, hide me always and shield me
under the shadow of your wings.

TODAY'S MORNING READING: Proverbs 27:1–13

DAY 27

Wisdom Verse

"The refining pot is for silver and the furnace for gold, and a man is valued by what others say of him." —Proverbs 27:21

AN AMAZING FACT: If you gathered up all the gold on earth that has ever been refined, it would fit in a cube measuring only 65.5 feet on each side.

Did you know that gold refining dates back almost to the beginning of recorded history? Of course, the chemical and electrolytic methods used in today's refineries to separate gold from impurities are pretty complex compared to ancient methods. In one of the oldest processes, gold was crushed, ground to a powder, rinsed, mixed with a few simple ingredients—salt, bran, and lead—and heated in a crucible, or refining pot, for several days. The result was pure gold.

Just as precious metals are tested by the refiner, our characters are tested by God. The Revised Version translates our verse this evening in this way: "The fining pot is for silver, and the furnace for gold, and a man is tried by his praise." In other words, a person is tested by how he reacts to praise.

Of course, people's reactions vary, but a natural response to praise would be to feel a bit puffed up, somewhat proud. "Wow! I did okay, didn't I? I must be pretty good! I am rather superior, aren't I?"

Someone once said, "Talent is God-given. Be humble. Fame is man-given. Be grateful. Conceit is self-given. Be careful." Good advice, don't you think?

Now, there's nothing wrong with being happy and satisfied with a job well done. And there's nothing wrong with accepting praise—as long as you don't inflate yourself with it! Compliments are like perfume: to be sniffed but not swallowed. As Christians, we know that every good gift, every talent, every ability, every opportunity, and every success is a gift from God.

Actually, there is a type of praise that we should crave—the praise that comes from God. The Bible tells us that when Jesus was on earth, many of the church leaders believed in Him but wouldn't acknowledge their faith, "for they loved the praise of men more than the praise of God" (John 12:43). They were proud. And pride—the source of the first sin—is one of the impurities that needs to be refined from our characters.

So what is our reaction to praise? Do we swell inside with pride in ourselves, or do we acknowledge the goodness of God in making our success possible? Our response to this test tells volumes about the quality of our characters.

> *Dear Father, please purify me and make my character*
> *like that of Jesus, who shines brighter than pure gold.*

TODAY'S EVENING READING: Proverbs 27:14–27

DAY 28

Wisdom Verse

*"He who covers his sins will not prosper, but whoever confesses
and forsakes them will have mercy." —Proverbs 28:13*

AN AMAZING FACT: Not long ago, police in Zambia recovered stolen
money that had been buried on a man's farm. The value of the money
in American dollars was about $450,000,000!

How could a man living in one of the poorer regions of the
world gain access to that much cash? The answer is simple:
He worked for the government as labor minister. During a
search at the man's farm, authorities located two trunks crammed full of
money. They had been buried and covered over with a layer of concrete.
Naturally, the man was arrested and sentenced to prison.

In one way or another, people have been trying to bury their sins
for a very long time. Cain tried to cover up the murder of his brother
by feigning ignorance, but God already knew every detail of the crime.
Moses buried in sand the Egyptian he had murdered. But he couldn't
hide the truth of what he had done and soon had to flee for his life. King
David had Uriah killed in order to cover up his illicit relationship with
the faithful soldier's wife, but he couldn't hide anything from God or His
prophet. These men all paid a high price for trying to cover their sins!

Moses said, "Your sin will find you out" (Numbers 32:23). So why
do people think they can hide anything from the One who is all-seeing—
"He who searches the hearts," He who "knows all things"? (Romans 8:27;
1 John 3:20). That might be a hard question to answer, but one thing is for

certain: Trying to hide wrongdoing instead of confessing it and turning away only makes matters worse, especially in the offender's heart.

David describes this grueling situation in Psalm 32: "When I kept silent, my bones grew old through my groaning all the day long. For day and night Your hand was heavy upon me; my vitality was turned into the drought of summer" (vv. 3, 4). It sounds like refusing to repent cost him some miserable days and sleepless nights.

But once confronted with his sins, David made the right choice. He says, "I acknowledged my sin to You, and my iniquity I have not hidden. I said, 'I will confess my transgressions to the LORD,' and You forgave the iniquity of my sin" (Psalm 32:5).

The same forgiveness that brought such great relief to King David is available to anyone. God's Word assures us that any person who confesses and forsakes sins will have mercy.

Dear Lord, thank you for being my merciful Forgiver—
my Cleanser—when I confess and forsake my sins.

TODAY'S MORNING READING: Proverbs 28:1–14

DAY 28

Wisdom Verse

*"He who gives to the poor will not lack, but he who hides
his eyes will have many curses." —Proverbs 28:27*

AN AMAZING FACT: Many of the poorest people on earth "survive"
on less than $1 per day.

It's a heartrending fact that more than a billion people in the world
live in what is defined as "extreme poverty," lacking such basic
human needs as food, safe drinking water, shelter, and sanitation.
Education and medical care is out of the question for most of them. (And
we whine when our electricity goes off for a couple of hours!)

Jesus told us that we would always have the poor with us, and His
Word tells us that feeding and caring for them is our responsibility.
Sharing with others is part of God's plan for us. "But do not forget to
do good and to share, for with such sacrifices God is well pleased"
(Hebrews 13:16).

"He who hides his eyes," as if not looking at the problem will make
it go away, is doing wrong. It reminds me of the comment by Edmund
Burke: "The only thing necessary for evil to triumph is for good men to
do nothing." Some people are tempted to think they can turn a blind eye
and everything will be okay, or that they can leave the problem to others,
but Scripture tells us it's our obligation to help.

The apostle John wrote, "But whoever has this world's goods, and
sees his brother in need, and shuts up his heart from him, how does the
love of God abide in him?" (1 John 3:17). A person with God's love inside

cannot turn away from the desperate need of a fellow human being. Instead, "the righteous considers the cause of the poor" (Proverbs 29:7). And then he takes action!

It might seem that no matter how much we give, there are more people in need. And that's true. But it doesn't excuse us from doing what we can to help. We should help and keep helping. God promises a blessing to those who remember to care for the less fortunate. He says, "Blessed is he who considers the poor; the LORD will deliver him in time of trouble" (Psalm 41:1). Even the poor are blessed by giving to others. Remember the widow who put her two mites into the temple offering, or the widow in Zarephath who gave what would have been the last of her food to the prophet Elijah?

And don't forget Jesus' words that when we give to "the least of these"—food, water, clothing, shelter, caring—we are giving to Him.

Lord, open my eyes and my heart to the needs of others!

DAY 29

Wisdom Verse

"The king establishes the land by justice, but he who receives bribes overthrows it." —Proverbs 29:4

AN AMAZING FACT: Indonesia's President Suharto became known by the name "Mr. Twenty-Five Percent," because he only approved contracts that provided him 25 percent of the profit.

I think we all know that Indonesia isn't the only place on earth infected with government corruption. One of the most prevalent types of corruption in government is called a "kickback," a form of negotiated bribery where a government employee helps secure an inflated payment for goods or services that are not needed or sometimes of inferior quality. In return, they receive payment in the form of services, cash, merchandise, or favors.

Even doctors haven't been immune to the temptation. Until the Anti-Kickback Act was passed in 1987, many doctors sent Medicare patients to medical providers for treatments and tests they didn't need. Why? Because these providers secretly reimbursed the doctors for sending them business.

In case you think I'm only picking on politicians and doctors, many of us struggle at some point with resisting some form of bribery. It's part of our "old man" nature, and we get an early start. Children commonly try to bribe their friends, siblings, and parents. The Bible is full of examples of bribery as well. Think of Jacob, who took advantage of his brother's hunger and bribed him for the birthright. The payoff was a bowl of stew.

Bribery (along with his own poor choices) caused the ruin of Samson. When the Philistine lords came to Delilah, they said, "Entice him, and find out where his great strength lies, and by what means we may overpower him, that we may bind him to afflict him; and every one of us will give you eleven hundred pieces of silver" (Judges 16:5). That must have been a lot of money! She took the bribe, and poor Samson took the bait. And who could forget Zacchaeus? He was a Publican, or tax collector, a group hated by most because of their habits of cheating and using bribery to increase their wealth. But meeting Jesus turned his life completely around. And that's the key!

Our verse this morning suggests that if a ruler accepts bribes, his land is headed for ruin. That's not hard to believe. Whether on the giving or receiving end, participating in a bribe corrupts a person. Involving selfish desire and deceit, it violates trust and bolsters greed. The Bible speaks powerfully against this dishonest practice: "A bribe blinds the discerning and perverts the words of the righteous" (Exodus 23:8), and, "A bribe debases the heart" (Ecclesiastes 7:7).

Dear God, help me to resist any temptation for illicit
gain and to conduct my life with honesty.

TODAY'S MORNING READING: Proverbs 29:1–13

DAY 29

Wisdom Verse

"The fear of man brings a snare, but whoever trusts
in the LORD shall be safe." —Proverbs 28:27

AN AMAZING FACT: More than 70 million Christians have died as martyrs for their faith.

Y ou might be surprised to learn that more than half of these Christian martyrs died in the 20th century. We tend to think of martyrs as people who lived in ages past—people like Stephen of the early church period or Huss, Tyndale, Knox, and so many others of the Reformation era. But, in reality, Christians today are dying for their faith in huge numbers.

Some estimate an average of more than 280 Christians die for their faith every day, or about one every five minutes. These statistics only count Christians who were killed because they were Christians, and not those who happened to be victims of war.

It takes extreme courage for people to stand firm in their faith in the face of violent persecution, especially if it means surrendering their lives. This kind of courage can only come from God.

Fear of man is a trap that many people fall into; even such champions of faith as Abraham and Elijah fell prey to this type of fear at some point in their lives. When we fear other people, it makes us vulnerable. We live in dread of what others might think about us or do to us. The solution is a deep fear, or respect, for God. We need to live our lives with deep reverence for our Father in heaven, serving only Him, and paying more attention to what God says than to what anyone else says.

"Whoever trusts in the LORD shall be safe" doesn't mean that there won't be trials, persecution, or even death. It means that, in the end, God will redeem the ones who trust in Him. "The LORD redeems the soul of His servants, and none of those who trust in Him shall be condemned" (Psalm 34:22), "neither shall anyone snatch them out of My hand" (John 10:28).

The psalmist writes, "The LORD is on my side; I will not fear. What can man do to me?" (Psalm 118:6). Along the same lines, Jesus said, "And do not fear those who kill the body but cannot kill the soul. But rather fear Him who is able to destroy both soul and body in hell" (Matthew 10:28). In the end, only God deserves our fear and worship.

Dear Lord, keep me from being ensnared by a fear of
man. May I fear only you and be always faithful.

TODAY'S EVENING READING: Proverbs 29:14–27

DAY 30

Wisdom Verses

"Every word of God is pure; He is a shield to those who put their trust in Him. Do not add to His words, lest He rebuke you, and you be found a liar." —Proverbs 30:5, 6

AN AMAZING FACT: The estimated value of a complete copy of the original Gutenberg Bible is a staggering $30 million. Individual pages sell for as much as $20,000 to $100,000!

The Gutenberg Bible, first printed in 1454, was the first major book ever printed with moveable metal type in the Western world. Before this Bible was created, books had to be printed from wood blocks engraved with letters or copied out by hand. Sometimes this took many years to finish.

Johannes Gutenberg was the first European to print with moveable type. This ingenious man also invented the printing press, which he used to print the now-famous Bible. Gutenberg's Bible contains 1,272 pages. Rubrics, or decorative headings, were hand painted on some of the copies of the Bible, and the quality of the multi-color printing was excellent. Some people consider the Gutenberg Bible one of the most beautiful books in the world.

Sadly, out of more than 150 original copies, only 49 copies of this Bible are known to exist and, of those, only 21 are complete. While most of the copies are in Europe, several are in North America and several more in other parts of the world.

As impressive, important, and valuable as the Gutenberg Bible is, the words contained inside it are the real treasure. These are "the Holy

Scriptures, which are able to make you wise for salvation through faith which is in Christ Jesus" (2 Timothy 3:15). The ultimate purpose of the Bible is to help us find salvation.

There is a warning in our verse for this morning: "Do not add to His words, lest He rebuke you, and you be found a liar" (v. 6). Some people "tweak" the Scriptures to suit their own purpose. But we should be careful never to misquote, alter, or twist the meaning of Bible passages.

Our verse also tells us that "every word of God is pure." This is similar to the psalm that reads, "The words of the LORD are pure words, like silver tried in a furnace of earth, purified seven times" (Psalm 12:6). Because the Scriptures contain the purest truth in the universe—the very words of God—we can put our complete trust in what the Bible says.

> *My Lord, thank you for the precious message of*
> *salvation you have given me in your precious Word.*

TODAY'S MORNING READING: Proverbs 30:1–16

DAY 30

Wisdom Verse

*"The ants are a people not strong, yet they prepare
their food in the summer." —Proverbs 30:25*

AN AMAZING FACT: Some ants live in super colonies that contain
more than 300 million individuals.

Perhaps you have heard of the famous "parasol" or "leaf-cutter"
ants that make gardens and raise their own crops! These
amazing creatures are often seen walking in processions, each
one holding a piece of green leaf above its head! These bits of green leaf
are *not* for food, but are taken to their nests and made into a compost
soil—for these ants are actually *farmers*. They deliberately sow, prune,
fertilize, weed, harvest, and store a fungus crop as carefully as any
gardener tends his vegetables.

Some ants living in Texas clear a "field" of one or two square yards
and then plant rice. They lay out the rice in beds with pathways running
among the plants, and they keep their rice fields carefully weeded. When
the rice seeds ripen, the ants harvest them, remove the husks, and store
the kernels for food. Later, the ants with very large jaws crack the seeds
and crush the kernels into meal for the rest of the ants. If the rice gets
damp and is in danger of spoiling, other ants have the sole responsibility
of carrying the damp grain out into the sunshine for drying.

There are thousands of amazing scenarios to be found among the
roughly 10,000 species of ants on earth, and probably many thousands of
lessons to be learned from this tiny creature. In fact, the Bible calls the

lowly ant, which typically prepares in advance for the colder months, "exceedingly wise."

It's important for us to store the bread of life in our minds and be prepared in advance when it comes to our relationship with God. As a Christian, you always need to "be prepared to give an answer to everyone who asks you to give the reason for the hope that you have" (1 Peter 3:15 NIV). And we should be "sanctified and useful for the Master, prepared for every good work" (2 Timothy 2:21).

Most important, we need to be prepared to meet the Lord when He returns. In Jesus' story of the wise and foolish virgins, only five of them carried extra oil along with them and were ready to meet the bridegroom when He arrived at an unexpected hour.

Jesus said, "I go to prepare a place for you. And if I go and prepare a place for you, I will come again and receive you to Myself; that where I am, there you may be also" (John 14:2, 3). The Lord has prepared to receive us into His awesome presence. Are we prepared to go home with Him?

> *Father in heaven, give me the oil of your Holy*
> *Spirit and make me wise. Help me be prepared*
> *to meet my Savior at His soon return.*

TODAY'S EVENING READING: Proverbs 30:17–33

Wisdom Verses

"It is not for kings to drink wine, nor for princes intoxicating drink; lest they drink and forget the law, and pervert the justice of all the afflicted." —Proverbs 31:4, 5

AN AMAZING FACT: Americans spend close to $200 million on alcoholic drinks every day.

Politicians, as a whole, have a reputation for drinking alcoholic beverages.

Several presidents of the United States have been heavy drinkers. Martin Van Buren was nicknamed "Blue Whiskey Van" because of his ability to drink large amounts of alcohol without showing signs of drunkenness. Andrew Jackson, Franklin Pierce, and James Buchanan were also known to drink heavily. Grover Cleveland suffered stomach problems from an excess of alcohol.

On a more pleasant note, our country has had several presidents who were teetotalers for at least part of their lives. William Harrison, Millard Fillmore, Abraham Lincoln, William H. Taft, and Rutherford B. Hayes reportedly were non-drinkers, as were Calvin Coolidge, Jimmy Carter, and George W. Bush.

As we saw earlier, the Bible clearly prohibits the use of alcoholic drinks, but the Scripture has a special warning for those in leadership positions: "It is not for kings to drink wine, nor for princes intoxicating drink; lest they drink and forget the law, and pervert the justice of all the afflicted" (Proverbs 31:4, 5). There is more at stake when there is alcohol use by those in positions of authority—whether you're a president, a pastor, or the head of a family.

Isaiah also warns against a perversion of justice by rulers who drink. He writes, "Woe to men mighty at drinking wine, woe to men valiant for mixing intoxicating drink, who justify the wicked for a bribe, and take away justice from the righteous man!" (Isaiah 5:22, 23).

Paul says, "And do not get drunk with wine, for that is dissipation, but be filled with the Spirit" (Ephesians 5:18 NASB). Even a "social drinker" can cause a perversion of justice. Just consider the fact that one drink can cause a person to become "legally drunk." If they're not fit to drive, how can they be fit to make and interpret laws? How can they render justice in a legal setting?

God is concerned for the afflicted. He wants them to get a fair trial; He wants them to receive justice. The best course for people in authority—as well as the rest of us—is to refrain from using alcoholic drinks and serve with a clear mind.

Father, please help those in leadership positions to resist the temptation of alcohol and avoid the perversion that follows it.

TODAY'S MORNING READING: Proverbs 31:1–9

DAY 31

Wisdom Verses

"She considers a field and buys it; from her profits she
plants a vineyard. She girds herself with strength, and
strengthens her arms." —Proverbs 31:19, 20

AN AMAZING FACT: There are more than 8,000 varieties of grapes
that come in an astonishing variety of colors: purple, blue, white, red,
golden, green, and black, each with a unique flavor.

The average American eats about eight pounds of grapes every
year. The oldest cultivated grapes in America are about 400
years old, brought here by Spanish explorers. A single grapevine
can grow up to 50 feet in length and produce 15 to 20 pounds of grapes
in a growing season.

The virtuous woman described in our final chapter is incredibly
industrious, a virtual superwoman. That's because she is a beautiful
analogy for the church, the bride of Christ.

Notice some of the things she does: She buys a field and "from her
profits she plants a vineyard" (Proverbs 31:19). Grapes in the Bible are a
symbol for the blood of Christ or the gospel.

Let's look at some of the projects she tackles: "She seeks wool and
flax, and willingly works with her hands; the church should be covering
the lost with the robe of Christ's righteousness. She provides food for her
household ... considers a field and buys it ... plants a vineyard ... stretches
out her hands to the distaff, and her hand holds the spindle ... all her
household is clothed with scarlet ... makes tapestry for herself ... makes

linen garments and sells them, and supplies sashes for the merchants" (vv. 13, 15, 16, 19, 21, 22, 24). Whew! This lady is a whirlwind!

One thing clearly stands out: She seems to be very successful in everything she does. What makes her so successful? The first clue is in the way she treats her husband, a type of Christ. "She does him good and not evil all the days of her life" (v. 12). The next clue is in verse 20: "She extends her hand to the poor, yes, she reaches out her hands to the needy." (The church should be ministering to the poor.) Further down we read, "She opens her mouth with wisdom, and on her tongue is the law of kindness. (The word and wisdom of God should be found among His people.) She watches over the ways of her household, and does not eat the bread of idleness" (vv. 26, 27).

Most important, she is "a woman who fears the LORD" (v. 30).

Dear Lord, please help me to be faithful,
industrious, kind, and God-fearing.

TODAY'S EVENING READING: Proverbs 31:10–31

129

NOTES

NOTES

NOTES

NOTES

NOTES

NOTES

NOTES

NOTES

NOTES

NOTES

NOTES

NOTES